HAPPY

MW01205589

Third Grade Reading Lessons

Second Edition

by

Edna K. Wenger

CHRISTIAN LIGHT PUBLICATIONS, INC.
Harrisonburg, Virginia 22801

Christian Light Publications, Inc., Harrisonburg, Virginia 22801
© 1954 by the Textbook Committee, Lancaster Mennonite Conference.
© 1977 by Christian Light Publications, Inc.
All rights reserved. First edition 1954
Second edition 1977
Printed in the United States of America

07 06 05 04 03 02 01 00 99 98   8 7 6 5 4

ISBN 0-87813-912-5

PREFACE

The children in our homes bring to us a challenge that needs to be met by proper nurture. Christian parents will want their children to grow up under Christian influences. The Christian day school is a part of the program that is intended to meet this challenge.

An important element in the work of the Christian day school is the reading material that is put into the child's hands. Reading materials with a Christian emphasis are needed in many subjects of the school curriculum. It is one thing to teach a course in reading or literature that is entirely free of error; and it is an entirely different thing to teach those courses with the Christian philosophy of life as the motive and reason for the courses.

There is a wide-open field of opportunity for the writer with ability and conviction to develop new materials in many areas. There is little good teaching material with an emphasis that is truly Christian. Some textbook writers have tried to avoid the problem by saying nothing for or against Christianity. They seek the patronage of Christians and non-Christians. Many texts, on the other hand, carry an emphasis that is definitely anti-Christian. These texts are poison to young minds. This situation should alert us to provide soundly Christian curriculum material.

This textbook is an effort to give our children character-building stories in place of the materials so commonly found in textbooks of the day. However, this book can also find a place in the literature of the Christian home, where parents are constantly looking for more good books for their children to read.

The stories in this reader have been prepared with the pupil of third grade reading ability in mind. Much of the material was written by Edna K. Wenger. She also edited the materials written by others. We sincerely appreciate the careful work and interest she put into this work. For several of the stories the editor turned to persons whose experiences and background gave them particular interest and ability to write these parts. We appreciate their work.

We also appreciate the contributions made by the persons who read the manuscript. Reviewers of the original edition were: John E. Lapp, Emily L. Kraybill, Esther K. Lehman, Katherine P. Graham, and Noah G. Good. Harold H. Brenneman supervised the original art and format.

For this Christian Light Publications reprint our thanks go to the original publishers for permission to reissue the volume. Roger Berry and Audrey Shank assisted in evaluating and reediting the book.

We gratefully acknowledge permission of the copyright owners to use the following: *The Miracle Baby*, China Inland Missions Publications; *Indian Children*, J. B. Lippincott and Frederick A. Stokes Company, Inc.; and, *The Little Black Sheep*, Christian Publications.

We prayerfully contribute this work to the boys and girls in our Christian day schools. We trust that the stories may have much value in character building and in learning to read. May the Lord add His blessing to this effort.

The Christian Day School
Editorial Committee
Sanford L. Shank
John D. Risser
John E. Hartzler

HAPPY LIFE STORIES

Stories

Stories

The Pet Squirrel

"Oh, Lois, come quickly," called Paul. "Come and see what I found."

Lois jumped off the porch swing where she was playing that she was riding in an airplane. She ran out to the orchard where Paul was standing under the big apple tree nearest the gate.

"What is it?" cried Lois. "It's a baby squirrel. Isn't it a tiny baby squirrel? Let me hold it, Paul. Do let me hold it."

"Be careful; it is very little. You might hurt it," said Paul. "I am going to ask Mother what to do with it."

"Baby squirrels ought to be with their mother," said the children's mother. "The mother squirrel feeds them and takes care of them. But I cannot see a squirrel's nest in the tree. Look! here is another baby squirrel. This one is dead. Perhaps the mother squirrel cannot take care of them.

Who will get me a little milk?"

"I will," said Lois.

"And who will bring the medicine dropper from the baby's table in the bathroom?"

"Let me get it," Paul said.

Soon Lois came with a little dish of milk and Paul came running with a medicine dropper. Mother took the medicine dropper and put a drop of milk on the baby squirrel's mouth. He was very hungry. Then Mother gave him another drop.

"Let me feed him, Mother," said Paul and Lois at once. They were so excited.

"Please, Mother, let me feed him."

"You may each feed him one drop of milk. Then we will put him in the house. You must treat him kindly. He is just a baby," Mother told the children.

Paul ran to the woodshed and got an old, round, wooden cheese box. Lois Ann got her torn old sweater from the ragbag on the attic steps.

"This will be a fine bed for our squirrel," said Lois Ann. "Here he can sleep and get well and strong."

Every day Paul and Lois Ann fed their pet squirrel. They fed him only a few drops each time. Each day the squirrel grew bigger. Soon he ran around in his old round cheese box. One day he jumped up and ran around the edge of the box. Then he jumped to the floor. He ran to Baby Ruth's feet and tickled them with his bushy tail. Baby Ruth laughed and laughed until she dropped the cookie she was eating. Then the squirrel ran to one of the crumbs. He nibbled at it with his little pointed mouth and his sharp white teeth.

"Look, Mother, the squirrel is eating Ruth's cookie crumbs," called Paul.

"We will have to feed him now," said Mother. "He is big enough to eat. Milk is for babies."

"He should have a name too," said Paul. "What shall his name be?"

"The squirrel in my reader is Grayling," said Lois Ann. "Call him Grayling."

"But he is not a gray squirrel. He is a red squirrel," said Paul. "Grayling will not do for a name for our squirrel."

"I heard of a squirrel called Nimble," said Mother. "That was a squirrel in our reading book when I was a little girl. But that is a hard name for Baby Ruth to say."

Just then Father came in for dinner.

"Father, we are trying to name our pet squirrel," said Lois Ann. "What would be a good name for our squirrel?"

"Let us think of some things he does," said Father.

"He runs very fast," said Paul.

"He drinks milk from a medicine dropper," said Lois Ann.

"This morning he ate a crumb from Baby Ruth's cookie," said Mother.

"And he tickled Ruth's bare feet with his bushy tail," said Lois Ann.

"Bushy-tail, Bushy-tail," said Baby Ruth, who tried to say everything that Lois said.

"That is a good name," said Father. "You could call him Bushy-tail."

"That is a good name for him," said Paul.

"I like it too," said Lois Ann. "Baby Ruth has named him Bushy-tail."

Every day Bushy-tail grew bigger.

"We cannot keep him in the kitchen," said Mother.

"I do not want a squirrel in my kitchen," said Mother. "He runs about on the chairs. He runs across the work table. Yesterday he ran around above the windows. You must find another place for him."

"We could keep him in the barn. Then he could run around in the hay mow and on the logs and lots of other places," said

Lois Ann.

"Oh, no," Paul said. "The cats would get him. He cannot live in the barn."

Just then John came in. John was the hired boy who worked for Father. Paul and Lois Ann asked him where they could find a home for Bushy-tail.

"I'm not afraid of a squirrel," said John. "If Mother says so you may keep him in my room. He will be good company. I'll feed him peanuts."

"If John doesn't care, I am sure I don't," Mother said.

Often John fed Bushy-tail peanuts. Once Mother gave Lois Ann a tiny piece of spice cake for Bushy-tail. Bushy-tail liked spice cake very much. One day Paul asked Mother why Bushy-tail would always carry a nut or a piece of cake back of the dresser to eat it, and then would come back for more. Mother told Paul that Bushy-tail liked to store pieces of cake or nuts. She told the children that all squirrels store nuts away for the winter and that God had made squirrels like that. Even though Bushy-tail was fed often, he still tried to save some food for the winter.

Autumn was coming. The asters in the garden were blooming, purple and pink and white. The Virginia Creeper at the porch was getting deep red. Along the road golden rod was blooming. One day the children saw that the school house was open. Two women with buckets and brooms and brushes were cleaning it. Mother had bought Paul and Lois Ann each a very big hollow pencil filled with pencils of all colors.

Father said, "Children, next week you will need to go to school. What do you think we should do with Bushy-tail? He is a big squirrel now. Do you think he would like a tree for a home better than John's bedroom?"

"What would Bushy-tail eat?" said Lois Ann. "Mother and I cleaned out all his nuts and cakes from behind John's dresser."

"The oak tree in the north field is full of acorns," said Paul. "And the walnut trees have many more walnuts than we need. Bushy-tail could have some."

"He will take care of that," said Mother. "That is how God made him. God made squirrels so that they like the woods and orchards better than our houses."

"Let us take Bushy-tail out to the oak tree far up in the north field," said Paul. "Come, Lois Ann."

So Lois Ann and Paul took Bushy-tail out to the north field. Lois Ann carried Bushy-tail and Paul pulled Baby Ruth in the wagon. They went up the long back lane, past the place where the wild strawberries grew, past the walnut stump, and out by the potato field to the line fence

where the oak tree was.

Paul held Bushy-tail a long time. Then he put him on the lowest branch of the big oak tree. Bushy-tail ran on the branch and far up the tree trunk.

"Good-by, Bushy," called the children.

But Bushy-tail only ran higher up into the branches.

Every day the children went to see Bushy-tail. Every day Bushy-tail would come and take cake from their hands. Soon school started. The children had lessons to do in the evenings. One Saturday Paul said, "Lois, let's go to see Bushy. We didn't go at all this week."

Paul and Lois Ann each took a crumb of spice cake and went up the back lane, past the wild strawberries, past the walnut tree at the hill top, and through the level potato field where the men were picking up potatoes. They went on to the oak tree in the north field.

The children called and called. Soon they saw a bushy red tail in the green leaves. But Bushy-tail would not come for the crumb of cake.

"I will put it in this fork of the tree," said Paul. "Then Bushy-tail can get it. Let's watch him."

Bushy-tail looked all around with his bright and beautiful eyes. At last he took a crumb in his mouth and ran up the tree.

The children did not see where he put it. Then he came back for the other crumb. He ate it sitting on his hind legs and holding it between his front paws.

"Bushy-tail likes his tree home," Paul told Father that evening. "I am glad we let him go."

"God made squirrels to be wild and free," said Father. "They are happier that way. You can still go to see Bushy-tail whenever you want to, and you can give him food too, but I am sure he is able to take care of that himself. He is a big squirrel now."

A Trip to the Planetarium

Lois Ann and Paul were so happy that they did not know what to do. Uncle Dan had told them that on Paul's birthday he would give him a birthday present and that he would give Lois Ann her present on the same day. Lois Ann's birthday would come in October but she was going to have her present on Paul's birthday.

Soon they saw Uncle Dan's car turning in the long lane, and they ran out to the barnyard to meet him. Then Uncle Dan told them the secret. Their birthday present was to be a train ride. Lois Ann and Paul had never had a train ride before and they were so glad that they did not know what to say at first.

"Oh, Uncle Dan! How could you ever think of such a wonderful present?" Lois Ann said at last.

"Thank you! Thank you!" Paul said again

and again.

Uncle Dan talked to Father and Mother and gave Baby Ruth a big red and blue ball with a doll face on it. Lois Ann and Paul put on their good clothes. Then Uncle Dan got into the car behind the wheel, and Lois Ann and Paul jumped in beside him. They drove down the lane and up the road toward the town. At last they came to the town. At the third traffic light, Uncle Dan turned right and drove out to the railroad station at the edge of town. After he had parked the car, he locked all the doors and put the key in his pocket.

The children walked up the marble steps to the station with Uncle Dan.

At the ticket window, Uncle Dan said, "Three round-trip tickets to Philadelphia."

The children watched the ticket agent stamping the three yellow tickets. He pushed them through the bars and gave Uncle Dan his change. Uncle Dan and Lois Ann and Paul walked back through the station until they came to a red sign with yellow letters that said, "To Philadelphia." They went down the steps to the platform beside the train tracks. One train whizzed by so fast that the children could hardly see the people in it.

"How could anyone ever get on that

train?" Paul asked. "It is so far away from the platform."

"That train does not stop in this town. It goes very fast and stops only in the big cities," Uncle Dan told the children.

Soon the children heard the announcer calling, "East-bound train, number 608, Philadelphia, New York, coming in on track one."

Soon they saw the engine coming around the bend. Slower and slower the train came until it stopped altogether. The doors opened and people began to come out of the cars. Uncle Dan waited until no one came out of the door near where they stood. Then he and the children stepped onto the platform of the car. They found two empty seats. He pushed the back of his seat to the front and sat facing the children.

Soon the train began to move, very slowly at first and then more rapidly. It went above the river on a high iron bridge and through a tunnel under the highway. Uncle Dan showed the children many things along the way. He showed them a large steel mill where hundreds of men work and where they could see big cranes lifting heavy loads of steel.

They saw many trees. Lois Ann told Uncle Dan that she thought the tall, straight trees with yellowish-green flowers were tulip trees. Uncle Dan said she was right. He told the children to look at the beautiful trees with deep purple leaves and gray bark like elephant's hide. "Those are purple beech trees," he said. "The bark is just like the bark of the beech trees in Hess's woods at home, only the leaves are purple. That is why they are called purple beeches." Along the rivers they saw many gray trees with big white spots on the bark and little furry balls hanging on the branches. Paul and Lois

Ann knew that they were sycamore trees. Beautiful roses were blooming in the lawns, and along the banks great honeysuckle vines with their yellow and white blossoms were climbing. Because all the windows were closed, Lois Ann and Paul could not smell the sweet flowers.

The train went by rows and rows of brick buildings and Uncle Dan told them that they were coming into the city. Far down on the streets the trucks and cars went rolling by. Slowly the train rolled into the first station, but Uncle Dan told the children that they would get off at the second station. In a few minutes they reached their station, and Uncle Dan and the children walked down the aisle and stepped onto the long platform. Crowds of people were walking in every direction. Uncle Dan took Paul's hand in his right hand and Lois's in his left hand and walked rapidly toward the steps. Soon they came out of the station to the busy street.

"I am hungry," Uncle Dan said. "It is almost my dinner time. Perhaps we should eat first and then go to the Franklin Institute."

Just across the street was a building with a large lighted sign in front. This was where Uncle Dan said they would eat. Inside this building and along the sides were many little glass doors. Inside each door was a little shelf, and on the shelf they saw many good things to eat. There was milk in little bottles. There were sandwiches, cake, fruit, meat, vegetables, and pie. Lois Ann and Paul watched people put money into little slots, turn a handle, and get pie or cake or sandwiches. Uncle Dan gave them each some nickels and some dimes to get their dinner. He gave them each a tray on which to put the food. They pushed the tray along a smooth shining rail. When they came to the end of the rail, Uncle Dan told the children to follow him to a little table near the window. They quietly bowed their heads to ask God's blessing on the food. All around them many other people were eating their lunch too. Out on the street they could hear the roar of hundreds of cars and busses.

When Uncle Dan and the children had finished lunch, it was twelve o'clock. They walked down the street and crossed at the busy crossing, and walked about a block until they came to a wide street.

"In that building is the planetarium, but there are many other things to see too. We will not go to the zoo this time because you were there last year," said Uncle Dan.

Before the planetarium opened Uncle Dan showed Lois Ann and Paul many things. In one room was a big locomotive into which you could climb and go for a very, very short ride. Lois Ann and Paul went with Uncle Dan into the cab of the locomotive. One man put a penny on the track for the wheels to go over. When Paul climbed down the steps he gave him the flat penny.

The children saw a long bicycle with seven seats and seven pairs of pedals.

"All the third grade children in our school could ride on that bicycle at one

time," Lois Ann said.

In one room was a car in which people could sit and drive. Only the car remained still. It looked as if traffic were moving in all directions. Uncle Dan sat in the car and pretended to drive very carefully, just as if the traffic were real. When he was finished he got a little card which told him what kind of a driver he was. Uncle Dan laughed when he saw the card. He had made no mistakes. He was a careful driver.

It was two o'clock and time to see the planetarium. The three friends walked through the hall to a door where there was a big glass globe with golden stars painted on it. About sixty other children and a few grown people were waiting at the door. A man at the door took the tickets and the people found seats in the large, round room with the dome-shaped ceiling. Outlines of the tops of buildings were painted on the wall. These, Uncle Dan told the children, are paintings of the tops of buildings in Philadelphia. He showed them the big statue of William Penn on city hall and the dome of a large church.

In the center of the room stood the planetarium, the large machine which caused the stars to appear on the sky. As the man behind the desk began to talk, the room grew darker and darker. He told the people that they would have to wait until they had cat eyes, that is, until they were used to the darkness. At last when the room was quite dark, the speaker pressed the button which started the planetarium. Suddenly, all the sky was filled with beautiful stars. It looked like a starry night far out in the country. The speaker said that this is the way God made the stars and that they had never changed.

"This is how the sky will look this evening," the speaker told the people. "See if you can find some stars and star groups. What is this?"

An arrow pointed to a group of stars. It was shaped like a dipper.

Then the speaker pointed to a star directly above the pointers of the dipper and told the children that it was the North Star. He told the children that if they knew the North Star they would never be lost. The speaker came back to the Big Dipper. He told the children that in France, the people say it is a saucepan. Long ago in England they called it a wagon. Now English children call it the plow. The Greek and Roman children called it the big bear.

In the west he showed the children the planet Saturn with its rings. Then he showed the children a group of stars shaped like a little crown. He told them that was Corona, the crown, and that the bright star was the gem in the crown.

After a while he made the stars move very rapidly. He showed them the planet called Orion, the hunter, and told them that they could read about Orion in the Bible. He showed them the group of stars shaped like a "V" and told them they were the Hyades. He showed them a very tiny group of stars called the Seven Sisters. He showed them the group of stars called the Big Dog and the group of stars called the Little Dog.

When the speaker was finished, the stars disappeared. Then he asked the children if they had any questions. One little boy asked how the speaker made the arrow point to the stars he wanted to show. The speaker showed him a flashlight with all the glass painted black except for a part shaped like an arrow. No other children asked any questions, and the group left the room where the planetarium was kept.

Uncle Dan asked the children if they

would like to have a ride on the electric train that went through the subway under the city and on the elevated track above the streets. He told them that he would take them thirty blocks to visit some of his friends who lived beside the church.

The children followed Uncle Dan down the cement steps to a long hall under the streets. The hall smelled damp like a cellar. At a little booth Uncle Dan gave a lady three dimes and each of them went through the gateway. Soon a train of five cars came roaring through the subway. Quickly Uncle Dan and the children went through the doors and found seats. Again the train stopped and people poured off to the platform. More people got on the train. Twice again the train stopped. Then it went shrieking around a corner and came out into the daylight. Uncle Dan told the children to look down on the streets. They were high above the streets and could look into the upstairs windows. Down below lay the beautiful river with a few boats on it.

Finally Uncle Dan told the children that they would get off the train at the next station. They stood by the door waiting until the train stopped. They went down the steps to the street below. The minister's wife welcomed them to her home. She told them that the minister would soon be there and she showed the children the clean little church and the rooms where the children had Sunday school. While Uncle Dan talked with the minister, Lois Ann and Paul played ball with James and Marie in the back yard with the high board fence around it.

Uncle Dan soon called the children and told them that they would have to leave to be in time for the train. They said good-bye to the kind minister and his wife and to James and Marie and walked up the street to the station.

They hurried back to the railroad station and soon they were stepping into the train that was to take them home. On the train Uncle Dan bought them sandwiches and milk. Before the children knew what had happened Uncle Dan was shaking them both. They rubbed their eyes and saw that they were back in the town where they had taken the train that morning. They had been so tired that they slept all the way home.

That evening two tired children jumped out of Uncle Dan's car very glad to be home with Father and Mother and Baby Ruth again.

"Thank you, Uncle Dan, for this wonderful birthday present," they called as he drove away.

How the Children Made Ink

"Look at those pretty purple berries! Are they good to eat?" Paul asked Mother as they were picking up apples in the orchard one autumn afternoon.

"Oh, no," Mother replied. "Those are pokeberries. Early in the spring when the leaves begin to push through the ground, some people gather these tender new leaves and cook them and eat them. The berries are food for birds, but people do not eat them. God has given them to the birds for food. If you will gather some of the berries, I will show you how to make ink from them. When I was a little girl we made ink out of pokeberries. Then we made pens from chicken feathers and wrote letters to each other with our feather pens and our pokeberry ink. You can write very beautifully with a feather pen."

"I know how to make a feather pen," Paul said. "Father showed us how. A feather pen is called a quill."

Paul helped Mother to carry the apples into the kitchen. Then he took a berry box from the summer kitchen and ran far out through the orchard to the place where he had seen the tall pokeberry bushes. Some of the bushes were taller than Paul and they had purple stems and big green leaves.

"I will gather only a cupful. I must leave the birds plenty of food," Paul thought as he gathered the bright berries.

The berries stained Paul's fingers a beautiful deep pink. Paul wondered whether the Indians used pokeberries in their war paint.

That evening, when Paul and Lois Ann had finished helping Mother weed the

garden, Paul took the pokeberries to
Mother. Mother gave Lois Ann a thin
white piece of old cheesecloth. Then she
told Paul to pour some of the berries into
the cloth. Below the cloth she set a little
white dish. She twisted the sides of the
cloth to form a little tight bag of pokeberries. Then she told Lois Ann to squeeze
the berries until the juice ran into the
dish. Soon the thick purple ink was drop-

ping into the dish. When Lois Ann opened the cloth, only seeds and berry hulls were in the bag. She threw the seeds and skins over the fence into the orchard and Paul poured more berries on the cloth. Lois Ann twisted the cloth into a little bag and squeezed it tightly. Soon more ink was dropping into the white dish. Paul found an empty ink bottle on the shelf in the play house. He washed it carefully and slowly Mother poured the thick juice into the bottle. At last Lois Ann had squeezed all the juice from the last berries. The children had nearly half a bottle of bright ink.

"Now we must have pens," said Lois Ann.

The children ran to the chicken house. Soon Lois Ann came in with one of a red chicken's big tail feathers. Paul found a gray and white feather that a Barred Rock rooster had lost. With a knife Mother sharpened the pointed ends carefully. On the back of an old envelope she wrote neatly, "Paul and Lois Ann made pokeberry ink from berries that grow in our orchard."

Then Lois Ann wrote her name and the numbers to twenty-five. Paul printed his name and wrote the numbers to twenty-five.

"May we write a letter to Aunt Rhoda this evening with our new ink?" the children asked.

"Yes, you may write with bright ink this time to show Aunt Rhoda what a beautiful color it is. But I will write the address outside the letter in blue ink. People should write letters in blue ink or in black ink and not in red ink and green ink. It is much easier to read and is not so hard on the eyes. This time you may write your letters with your bright ink, but after this remember to use blue ink or black ink."

"May we use our quill pens too?" asked

Paul.

"Yes, you may use your quills too. In your letter you may tell Aunt Rhoda what you learned about pokeberries today."

Building the Leaf Houses at School

The seven Norway maple trees in the school yard were sending their sap down into the roots for the winter. The teacher told the children that when the cold weather came the sap in the trees went back to the roots and the trees stopped making the green color which they made in the sunlight from part of the air. Then the leaves turned a pale yellow. Sugar maple trees turned bright orange. When Lois and Paul looked up the winding road to Hess's woods Mother said, "Look how bare the woods are. There are just a few colors. They look almost like the woods in the springtime when the leaves are little and new."

Out in the schoolyard in the morning at recess time, and at noon the boys and girls were busy. Paul, Dan, and John were helping the bigger boys to build a house of leaves in the fence corner at the far end of the schoolground. It would be a tractor house, the boys said. The big boys had made a frame of old boards from the woodhouse and the first and second grade boys were gathering leaves on a big open burlap bag. One boy held each corner and two boys were piling leaves high on the opened bag. Then the boys would run with their load of leaves down to the far end of the schoolyard where the third and fourth and fifth grade boys were stuffing the leaves into the open places in the frame. "Put-put-put," the first and second grade boys would say as they played they were a tractor hauling a heavy load of bricks. "Put-put-put." Allen and Ray, the big boys, were nailing burlap across the top for a roof. There were four little windows in the house and a door in front. The house was so high that all the boys except

Allen and Ray could stand up straight in it.

On the other side of the walk very near the schoolhouse the girls were making a playhouse. It had no roof and the leaf walls were very low, but it had a kitchen, a living room, and two bedrooms. It was to be a house for a family. Just as Lois was trying to nail a loose piece of wood, using a stone as a hammer, she looked up.

"Paul," she called, "don't take those leaves, they are the girls' leaves."

"Oh, no," called Dan. "This is our tree."

The six smaller boys were gathering leaves from the maple tree that stood in the middle of the schoolground. Three trees nearest the girls' playhouse belonged to the girls and they could have all their leaves, and the three trees on the other side were the boys' trees and they could have all those leaves, but no one was ever sure who should have the leaves from the middle trees.

"Our house is much bigger than yours," called John. "We will need more leaves. Your house doesn't have a roof. Its walls are low."

"But there are more girls than boys," one of the Hill twins said to her brother John.

"And we have four rooms and you have only one room," said the other twin.

Soon all the girls came out of their

playhouse to the trees where the twins and Lois Ann and the little boys were talking. Then down from the house where they were stuffing leaves in the frame came the third and fourth and fifth grade boys. Allen and Ray were busy on the roof and they just kept on piling leaves and laying small stones upon them.

Just then the school bell rang. All the children ran to the schoolhouse and sat in their seats, waiting for Sister Brown to begin the story hour. This was the story Sister Brown told the children:

"Where can I find grass for all my sheep?" Abram thought as he looked across the green pasture lands.

"There I can find grass for all my sheep if I can have all the land," thought Lot.

Soon Abram's servants and Lot's servants began to fight. Abram's servants wanted the best land for Abram, and Lot's servants wanted the best land for Lot.

Then Abram called Lot and said, "We won't be angry with each other. There is enough room for both. Look out over the pasture lands. Take what you want. If you go west, I shall go east. If you go east, I shall go west."

Because Lot wanted the best for himself, he took the rich east country near the river. Abram took what was left.

But God came to Abram and said, "Don't forget that some day I will give you all the land."

Then Abram believed God and worshiped Him.

Sister Brown finished the story, the schoolroom was very quiet. "Tick-tock, tick-tock," said the big clock high on the front wall of the schoolroom. Then the teacher said, "Boys and girls, with whose choice do you think God was pleased? All who think He was pleased with Lot's choice, raise hands."

Not one hand went up.

"How many think God was pleased with Abraham's choice?"

Every hand went up.

Then Sister Brown said, "When you boys and girls go out to build houses at recess time, don't forget Abraham and Lot. The first grade may come to class."

At recess time Sister Brown looked out the window. What do you think she saw? At the middle maple tree were Allen and Ray. They had a string and were measuring the ground.

Then Allen took a string from his pocket and tied one end to the fence. He tied another end to a stake that Ray hammered far into the ground on the opposite side of the tree. But Sister Brown saw that Allen and Ray had placed the string over on their side about a foot from the trunk of the tree. This gave the girls a bigger space and more leaves. A little later when Sister Brown came out to see how the leaf houses were coming, she saw that Lois Ann and Katie and Barbara were helping to throw leaves from their side to the bag that the first-grade boys were using to carry leaves.

That evening before they went home Sister Brown said, "I am glad to see that you remembered Abraham and Lot. God has given us these stories to show us how to live. Good evening, boys and girls."

And she rang the school bell as they walked out in neat rows.

The Little Yellow Pin

It was autumn. The leaves on the seven Norway maple trees around the little red brick schoolhouse were all yellow. Some leaves were lying thick on the ground and they made a pretty rustling sound when the children ran through them. When Lois Ann looked out the window she could see the leaves falling gently to the ground, softly like snowflakes. Lois Ann knew that tomorrow she and Paul would help John to pick the heaps of yellow corn into bushel baskets and that John would put them on the wagon and haul them to the corncrib with the tractor. She and Paul would sit on top of the yellow ears of corn and ride down the long, bumpy back lane to the corncrib.

Just then Sister Gray's voice said, "You may put your books away, children. It is time to go home."

Lois Ann saw Dickie go softly up to the teacher's desk and give something to her. Sister Gray held it up for the children to see. It was a little yellow pin that looked like gold.

"Who lost this little pin?" she asked.

No one answered. Lois Ann looked at the pin. It was a pretty little pin. She thought of her doll, Bess. How she wished she could have it to pin Bess's pink dress with the red rosebuds in it. No one wanted the pin.

Again Sister Gray asked, "Whose little yellow pin is this?"

Again there was no answer.

Slowly Lois Ann raised her hand and Sister Gray motioned to her to come to the desk for the pin. Lois Ann pinned the little yellow pin inside her pocket and got her lunch box and spelling book. After all the children had said, "Good evening," some ran down the road toward the east and some ran up the road toward the west. Katie and Barbara, the twins, asked Lois Ann to see the pin. Slowly she turned her pocket inside out so they could see it. But Lois Ann was not happy and she did not talk much that evening. At the lane Katie and Barbara said, "Good-bye" and ran down the road.

Lois Ann saw Mother in the summer kitchen squeezing purple juice through a bag to make good sweet grape jelly for the winter. But she didn't want to talk to Mother and she hurried up the steps to her room where she changed her pink gingham dress for her blue everyday one. She took off her shoes and set them in the closet and put her stockings in the wash basket on the attic steps. She ran up to the playhouse in the upstairs of the summer kitchen and pinned Bess's rosebud dress with the new yellow pin. But somehow she didn't want to play with Bess. She went to watch Mother pressing grapes through the bag, but somehow she didn't want to talk to Mother this evening. She asked Paul to go with her to the oak at the line fence to see Bushy-tail the squirrel, but Paul had other things to do. She tried to read in her Bible story book. She sat on the lower step of the summer kitchen, but she didn't feel like reading. That evening Mother had corn on the cob and good Summer Rambo apple sauce for supper, but Lois Ann could eat only half her ear of corn.

"Are you sick, Lois Ann?" asked Father.

"I'm not hungry," Lois Ann said, thinking of the little yellow pin Bess was wearing in her rosebud dress.

Paul ate three ears of corn spread with Mother's own butter. He took a big helping of apple sauce. After supper Paul and Lois Ann played horse-and-driver using long strings for reins and running up and down the garden paths and long cement walks. They played that the paths were roads. They had so much fun that Lois Ann almost forgot about her yellow pin.

At eight o'clock Mother told Lois Ann to take a bath and go to bed.

"This evening I will be busy picking lima beans," she said, "and I believe you are big enough to go to bed alone. Don't forget to pray before you go to bed."

Lois Ann decided not to take Bess to bed with her that night. She looked out the west window where the sun had made the sky all purple and red and gold. There were little breaks in the clouds. Lois Ann liked to think that they were windows into heaven and that if she would look a long time she might see into heaven. She wasn't afraid upstairs alone for she knew that God was there and that the angels watch over the children. She hunted the Book of Ephesians and read a verse in her

little Testament that she got with red tickets in Sunday school. The verse was her memory verse for Sunday school next Sunday: "Let him that stole steal no more."

When Lois knelt down by her clean white bed to pray, she kept thinking of the little yellow pin that wasn't hers on Bess's dress. She asked God to bless Father and

Mother and Paul, Baby Ruth, and John and Aunt Rhoda and the children in Africa, but she was not happy. God did not seem to be there. She climbed into bed and shut her eyes but she didn't sleep. Outside she could hear the crickets and locusts singing in the night. She heard John whistling as he closed the barnyard gate, and she could hear the chickens making soft cackling noises in the rain shelters in the orchard. She heard Mother talking softly to Baby Ruth who was awake in the night. She heard the striking of the chime clock that Father had given Mother long ago. It was playing the Westminster Chimes: one-two-three-four-five-six-seven-eight-nine-ten! She had been lying in her bed for almost two hours.

Lois Ann shut her eyes very tightly and played that she was counting sheep; she counted to five hundred and still she could not sleep. She heard the chime clock play two lines of the Westminster Chimes:

"We are the chimes

That mark the hours . . . "

Lois Ann sang softly to the tune of the chimes.

At last Lois Ann climbed slowly out of bed. She tiptoed across the room and across the hall to the door of Mother's room. She opened the door very slowly and called, "Mother."

"Mother," she said again.

This time she heard Mother's soft voice, "What do you want, Lois Ann? It isn't morning yet."

Lois Ann began to cry, and Mother tip-toed softly with Lois Ann to her room. She turned on the lamp that was shaped like a beautiful white rabbit. Then she sat on the little low chest in which they kept Lois Ann's clothes that were too small for her, for Baby Ruth to wear some day. Lois Ann sat beside Mother on the little low chest.

She told Mother the story of the little gold pin that Dickie had found on the playground and that when nobody had wanted the pin, she had raised her hand as if it were hers.

"Lois Ann, I am glad you told me about the pin. It was wrong to take the pin because it was not yours. The Bible calls that stealing. What do you think we should do about it? Who should we tell about it first of all?"

Lois Ann looked at the picture of little Samuel that hung near her bed and said, "I must tell God that I am sorry."

So they knelt beside Lois Ann's bed. First Lois Ann prayed asking God to forgive her for lying and for stealing the pin. Then Mother thanked God that He had forgiven Lois Ann.

"Now," said Mother, "what will we do with the pin?"

Lois Ann said, "I must take it back to

Sister Gray on Monday and tell her that it was not my pin."

"All right, now I think you can go to sleep," said Mother as she kissed her and tucked her into bed.

Lois Ann felt very happy and soon after Mother had closed the door she was fast asleep. When Lois Ann woke up the sun was shining though the leaves making pretty shadow patterns on the thin white curtains. She could hear the tractor put-putting in the field where John was haul-ing in the corn, and downstairs the clock chimed:

"We are the chimes
That mark the hours
Making them sweet
As chains of flowers."

One-two-three-four-five-six-seven-eight-nine-ten!

Lois Ann and Paul helped John in the cornfield that afternoon, and in the evening they went with Father and Mother to the store to help select sweaters and dresses and suits and toys for Christmas packages for the children in Europe. On the Lord's Day they went to Oak Shade Sunday School where Sister Layman told the children a wonderful story about a miracle baby. In the afternoon Father read some Bible stories out of the story book and they played summer Bible school in the orchard house a long time. In the evening they went to church again and heard Brother Weaver preaching about the Good Shepherd.

When Monday came, Lois Ann took the little yellow pin and pinned it inside the pocket of her blue dress. When Sister Gray's blue car drove up to the school, Lois Ann took her red lunch box and her spelling book and ran down the lane and out the road. She walked softly up to Sister Gray's desk and told her the story of the little yellow pin. She asked Sister Gray to forgive her. Sister Gray laid the pin on her desk and at noon she told Lois Ann's story to the children.

Still no one claimed the pin and Sister Gray said she would leave it on her desk to remind the children to tell the truth.

The Leaf Game

One day the teacher told the children that they would go for a hike in Smith's woods.

"Will all the children gather as many different leaves as you can?" she asked. "We want to play a leaf game when we come back to school."

It was September and the leaves were still green. There were many different kinds of trees in the woods near the school. The big boys and girls helped the little children to get leaves from the larger trees. At the edge of the creek jewel weed was blooming. When the children touched the seed pods they went "snap" and scattered seeds all around. The teacher told the children that jewel weeds scatter seeds like that.

Just then the children said, "Oh, Paul, your clothes are all full of beggar's ticks."

All the children in third grade started to pull the ticks off Paul's clothes. Then the teacher told the children that each tick was a seed and this was the plant's way of scattering seeds.

"I don't like this way of scattering seeds," said Paul. "I don't like to carry seeds for beggar's ticks."

"The maples have a very pretty way of carrying seeds," said Sister Plank. "Each seed has little wings and the wind takes the seeds a long way from the tree. Other seeds have wings too."

Soon the children had gathered many leaves and they followed Sister Plank to the schoolhouse. When all the children were in their seats, Sister Plank told them how to play the leaf game. "One child will lay a leaf on my desk. If he can, he will tell the name of it. If he can't tell the name, I will tell it. Then all the children who have a leaf like it will put their leaves on the same pile. We will see for which tree you have the most leaves and which children have found some leaves that many of you have not found. John, you may start."

John did not know the name of his leaf. Sister Plank said it was the leaf of the tulip tree at the corner where the roads met. Ten children laid tulip tree leaves on John's pile. Then John called, "Sara."

Sara laid a leaf on the desk.

"It looks like a mitten," laughed Lois Ann.

"Mine has its thumb on the other side," Katie said.

"Mine has two thumbs," laughed Barbara.

"And mine has no thumbs," Sister Plank said. "We make good pink tea from the roots of this tree. What is it?"

"It is sassafras," said Paul. "We have many sassafras trees in the corner of our orchard."

Tulip   Sassafras   Sycamore

Seven children laid a leaf on Sara's pile. Then Sara called on Katie. Katie laid a very big leaf on the desk.

"My tree had little balls on it, and it has gray and white bark," she said.

"That is a buttonwood," Ray said.

"Yes," said the teacher, "and some call it sycamore."

Then Sam brought one of his leaves. It was little and shiny and had tiny points like pins.

Pin Oak   Maple   Elm

"Father told me this is a pin oak," he said.

When Allen came up he had a leaf. A little drop of something white like milk hung on the broken stem. All the children had a leaf like this, for it came from the Norway maple trees in the schoolyard.

James had a leaf from the tree near the bridge.

"Its leaves are not alike on both sides and the tree is shaped like a vase of flowers," James said.

Three children had elm leaves.

One boys had a white-oak leaf. The teacher said you could tell it by the rounded corners and the little acorns.

There were black willow leaves from the tree where the children went wading in summer. There was a gingko leaf, shaped like a little fan, from Freeman's yard, and there were beech leaves from the tree that has gray bark like the elephant's hide.

The clock on the front wall said three-thirty. Sister Plank told the children that next day she would paste all the leaves on the board. Then they would name them. How many do you know?

The Girl the Indians Stole

Long, long ago, long before Grand-father was a little boy, Indian children lived in this land. Where you go to school little Indian boys and girls played in the forest. Where the barns and houses and fields are, deep forests stood. There were no towns with stores and factories and churches, only Indian wigwams and little corn fields among the green trees. At night bear and wildcats prowled around in the forest. Many deer and rabbits and other wild animals ran softly about.

When white people came to our land from across the waters, the Indians could not understand why they had come. They thought the white people were their enemies. But William Penn was kind to the Indians and they loved him. They knew that William Penn was their friend. Some white men were cruel to the Indians, and the Indians hated them. Some Indians thought all white men were cruel. Sometimes the Indians would kill fathers and mothers and carry the little children away. Sometimes they would burn the houses of the white people.

In a little house in the forest lived a Christian woman and her little baby girl named Regina. The woman prayed to God and read her Bible and tried to be kind and good. She wanted little Regina to learn to love Jesus and to be a Christian some day.

One day a sad thing happened. A band of Indians came into the home of this dear woman. Little Regina was sleeping soundly in her bed. The Indian braves looked at the sleeping child and decided to take her with them to their wigwams. The mother looked everywhere for her little girl. But nowhere could she find the child. The mother was very lonely without Regina. Often she prayed. Often she sang a

song in German. The song was this:
"Alone and yet not all alone,
Am I in this lone wilderness,
I find my Saviour always nigh,
He comes the weary hours to bless."
Years passed. Little Regina lived in a bark bigwam. She ate Indian corn and fish and deer meat. She learned to hoe corn and carry heavy loads on her back. She wore a dress of animal skins and had her

hair braided in long braids. She was a woman now.

One day the mother heard good news. Someone told her that many of the children whom the Indians had stolen long ago were coming home. Fathers and mothers were going to find their long-lost children. The neighbors begged the mother to go. At last she said she would go.

Many people had gathered together. The mother stood among the rest. Her face was old and wrinkled. Her hair was white, almost as white as the cap she wore on her head. She looked everywhere. No Regina was to be seen. Kind people tried to help her. They asked whether Regina had no marks on her skin that her mother remembered.

"No, she was a perfect child. She had no marks," the sad old mother answered.

Then someone had a good idea.

"Did you ever sing to your little girl?" he asked.

"Oh, yes," the tired mother said. "I often sang to her while she played on the floor of our house and when I put her to bed."

"Sing one of the old songs," said the man.

The old mother closed her eyes. Then she began to sing,

"Alone and yet not all alone,
Am I in this lone wilderness,
I find my Saviour always nigh,
He comes the weary hours to bless."

Suddenly there was a little cry. From the crowd rushed a white girl in Indian clothes. The old mother put her arms around the girl and wept for joy. At last God had brought her daughter back to her. The girl had never forgotten the song her mother sang when she played on the cabin floor.

The Man Who Saved His Enemy

Long, long ago in Holland lived a man who loved Jesus very much. His name was Dirk Willems. Many people who called themselves Christians did not obey God and love the Bible. But Dirk loved the Bible and wanted to do all that God told him to do. When Dirk was just a little baby, his parents took him to the big church and had him baptized. But Dirk was only a baby and did not know what the minister was doing. When Dirk grew up and became a Christian he wanted to be baptized. Dirk went to a friend's house. At this place where some other people had come to worship God, the minister poured water on Dirk's head and said, "I baptize you in the name of the Father, and the Son, and of the Holy Spirit." Dirk was happy because he had obeyed the Word of God.

But the rulers of the land were very angry because Dirk had been baptized again. In their town were men whom they paid to catch thieves and other bad people. They called these men thief-catchers. Because Dirk had obeyed God's Word, these rulers told a thief-catcher to catch Dirk and bring him to the town.

It was a cold winter day. There was ice on the rivers and lakes of Holland. But at some places the ice was thin. Dirk ran across the fields through ice and frost. The thief-catcher ran after him. At last Dirk came to a river. He ran across the river on top of the ice. The thief-catcher came right after him.

Then, crash! The ice broke and the thief-catcher fell into the cold river water. Dirk looked around. There was his enemy trying to get out of the water. What should

Dirk do? Should he run away and be safe? Then the thief-catcher would drown. But Dirk remembered Jesus. He remembered that Jesus told us to love our enemies. Dirk wanted to obey Jesus.

Dirk went back across the ice, back to the hole where the thief-catcher was. He took the hands of his enemy in his and pulled him out of the water. He let Dirk go and told the town master what had happened. He begged the town master to save Dirk's life.

But the town master said, "You said you would catch Dirk."

Sometime afterwards the thief-catcher was sent again to get Dirk. This time he caught Dirk and brought him back to the town. They took Dirk to the town judges. The men asked Dirk, "Were you baptized again?" Dirk could not lie. He replied that he was baptized at Peter Willem's house.

They asked Dirk, "Did you have church

in your house?"

Dirk could not lie. He said that he had had church in his house.

Then they asked him, "Did you let other people be baptized again at your house?"

Again Dirk answered, "Yes."

Then the men said, "The king of Holland does not want people to do these things. You must be punished. Then people will learn to obey the king. You must be burned with fire.

Dirk was not afraid to die for Jesus. As he stood there suffering for Jesus he prayed again and again to God. The wind carried his prayers far. Even the people in the town heard his prayers. Just before Dirk went to heaven, he asked God to take his soul. Then Dirk went to live with God forever. There he will always be happy.

The Man in the Tower

Another Christian from Holland who suffered for Christ was named Hans Brael. Hans, like Dirk Willems, believed in being baptized again. He also believed that a Christian must love his enemies at all times. Hans and his fellow Christians were called Anabaptists. Anabaptist means "a baptizer again."

One spring day Hans was returning home from a meeting with some other Anabaptists. About three miles from a large castle he met a judge and a police officer who asked him, "Where are you going and what have you been doing here?"

Hans replied, "I have been with my brethren."

"Are your brethren Anabaptists?" the officer asked.

"Yes," Hans replied.

When the judge heard that, he arrested Hans. He took Hans' belt and tied it around him and made him walk like a dog through the mud. They walked to the castle, nearly three miles away. Hans grew so tired that he fell in the field near the castle. The officer dragged Hans into the castle, took all his money from him, and put him in the castle prison.

The next day the lord of the castle talked with Hans. He askd Hans if he had been baptized two times. He asked Hans what he thought about the communion bread. The lord of the castle was not pleased with the answers Hans gave. Hans went back to the prison.

Eight days later the judge returned and asked Hans who his Anabaptist friends were. Hans knew that the judge wanted to put his friends in prison. Hans would not tell the names of his friends. Then the judge told Hans that they would hurt him if he would not tell. Still Hans did not tell. For a long time Hans had to bear much pain. But God was with him and helped him. At last the lady of the castle said that they should stop punishing Hans. Again and again men tried to get Hans to put away his faith in Jesus. But still Hans was true to God.

Finally they put Hans into a dark tower

80

of the castle. Hans could not see the sun and the moon. He could not see the beautiful trees and flowers and sky. When it was cooler, he knew it was night. When it was warmer, he knew that it was day. It was so damp in the tower that Hans' clothes soon wore out. Hans had only a blanket about him. He kept the collar of his shirt and hung it on the wall.

One time the soldiers took Hans out of the tower for a little while. But the light was so bright, it hurt Hans' eyes and he was glad to go back to the dim, dark tower again. In the tower were snakes and many insects. When he got a dish of soup, he had to eat it quickly, before the insects fell into it. On top of his pitcher he kept a big stone, so that the insects would not fall into it.

One day Hans got a message from one of his Christian friends. This friend asked Hans to send him some sign that he was well and true to God. Hans could not even send him a piece of straw for a sign, because there was nothing in the tower. At last he remembered his old collar on the wall. This Hans sent back to his Christian friend. The Christians felt very sorry for poor Hans and sent word that they would send him clothes or anything that he needed. But Hans knew that he would have to suffer again if they sent him clothes. He told them not to send him anything.

All the long, beautiful summer Hans lay in the tower. Then autumn came and cold weather. Men took Hans out of the tower and put him into another prison. They fastened one hand and one foot to a wooden frame. For more than half a year Hans had to stand all the time. When people would pass they would look at Hans and say unkind things about him.

One evening a servant came into the

castle with his keys. He was going to free Hans, but he could not find a key that would fit. Hans told the servant that he should not free him because he might suffer for it. Then the lady of the castle sent word that Hans might go free if he would do two things. He should say that he was wrong and he should let her men teach him. Hans could not do this. He was sure he was right. He wanted to be true to God.

When spring came, Hans was told that he must go to sea where he would be punished with whips. But first he had to learn to walk again, for he had been in prison almost two years. He had not seen the sun for more than a year. When Hans could walk, a servant was told to take him to the sea. But first the lady of the castle wished to see him. Hans told her never again to harm the Christians who love the Bible. The lady wept and told Hans she would never harm them again. Then she gave Hans some money for the journey.

For two days Hans and the servant traveled toward the sea. At an inn this bad servant drank so much wine that he slept a long time. While the bad servant slept, Hans opened the door of the room and locked it again. Then he opened the door of the house and locked it. Hans went out into the night. God went with him and brought him safely to his Christian friends. Once more Hans went about the land and preached the Word of God to his people.

How Great-Grandfather's Great-Grandfather Came to America

"Father, where did you live when you were a little boy?" asked Paul one evening.

"Over at Uncle David's where the big stone house and the old stone barn are," Father said. "My father lived there when he was a little boy and my grandfather lived there, too. Grandfather's grandfather lived there when he was a little boy."

"That must be a very old house," Lois Ann said.

"It is an old house," said Father. "But long ago there was another house there. That house has been gone many years, and this stone house stands near the place where the old house stood so long ago.

Great-grandfather's great-grandfather built the first house."

"Where did great-grandfather's great-grandfather live before that?" Paul asked.

"That is a long, long story," Father said.

"Let us call great-grandfather's great-grandfather Hans. He lived a long, long time ago in a beautiful country across the ocean. This country is called Switzerland. Times were hard in Switzerland. Often there was very little food for dinner and only a little wood to burn. Often there was war in the land and Hans did not want to fight. How he wished for a home in a land where he could be free to worship God.

"One day Hans heard wonderful news. Far across the ocean was a land called Penn's Woods. Here were acres and acres of woodland where men could build homes in the forest and clear land for farms. But most wonderful of all, here one could have freedom to worship God. William Penn had received this land from King Charles of England instead of money which the king owed his father. In some ways William Penn worshiped God like Hans and his friends, and he had invited them to come and build homes in America. William Penn had died and now his sons were owners of Penn's Woods. They too wanted people to build homes on their

land.

"Hans told his wife about the new home in America. He told her that the journey would be long, and that there would be hard work, but that in Penn's Woods there would be freedom. Maria told Hans that she would go with him to America.

"People from Holland said they would help the people from Switzerland to go to America. They got a ship for them and lent money to those who did not have enough money for the journey. Maria had to cry a little when she and Hans left their little home to go down to the river and get on the boat that would take them to Holland. On the boat were many friends who wanted to start a new home in Penn's Woods in America. In Holland they found a boat waiting at Rotterdam to take them across the ocean.

"It was a long journey across the blue Atlantic. Some days the sun shone brightly on the little waves, and on other days the boat rolled and tossed on the gray waves that splashed high on the side of the ship. Some people became very sick. A few of them never saw the shores of America. They died on the ship, and because they were Christians, they found a place much more beautiful then Penn's Woods.

"At last the ship came to the place where a wide river flowed into the ocean. The ship sailed up the river with its low and sandy banks until it came to a city with many red brick houses. These people met the tired Mennonites and gave them food and good beds to sleep in that night. They were people who believed as William Penn believed. They were called Friends or Quakers.

"But Hans and Maria were eager to find their new homes in the woodland. They wanted to build a house and plant some seeds before winter came again. The kind Quaker ladies gave the Mennonite women seeds to plant in their gardens. They could not take many things with them, for they were going to walk.

"The Mennonites said good-bye to their Quaker friends and started walking toward the west with a guide who knew the forest. The trees were very tall and wild flowers grew on the forest ground. Sometimes they had to climb steep hills and sometimes they walked in low valleys. Clear streams of water flowed through the forests and many times the travelers had a good meal of fish from the streams. It was a good land to which God was bringing these people.

"After some days they came to a broad valley. Here and there in the forest other Mennonites had built rough log houses. Some had already built houses of stone with great stone fireplaces in the center.

In these larger houses they gathered to worship God on the Lord's Day. For many years Mennonites had church in the houses of different families.

"Hans and Maria found a lovely place where a spring of clear cold water bubbled out of the ground. Here they built their first rough log house, and here Hans worked year after year clearing more and more land for their farm. Children were born and as soon as the boys grew old enough they helped Hans cut wheat with a sickle and tie the wheat into bundles. The girls learned to spin and to cook and to sew. The days were busy ones, and always there was freedom, freedom to worship God.

"One day Maria told Hans that the log house was very small. 'Our family is too big for it,' she said.

"From stone that they found on the limestone hill back of the barn, Hans and the boys began slowly to build the walls of a house. Sometimes neighbors would help. Week after week and month after month the house grew. Wood came from the forest and iron nails and hinges from the forge across the hills. On a stone above the door Hans cut the letters of his name and of Maria's. For many years Hans and Maria lived here. Years later, when their children were old men, the house that you see at Uncle David's was built. But out in the yard, if you would dig, you could find stones from the house that Hans and Maria built.

"Written on this sheep skin paper, you may see the permission that William Penn's sons gave to Hans and Maria to show them that the land was theirs. It is called a *deed*."

When Lois Ann and Paul went to Uncle David's farm with its cool, clear spring of water and its old stone house with the

wide, wide window sills, they remembered the story of Hans and Maria and
their home in Penn's Woods.

How the Martyr Book Was Made

It was late Sunday afternoon. For a long time Lois Ann and Paul had played church and Sunday school in the house in the orchard. But they were tired of playing now.

"Let's ask Father to tell us a story," Paul said. The children ran down the path and through the back yard gate to Father. Father looked up from the church paper he was reading and smiled.

"Guess what we want," laughed Lois Ann.

Father did not need to guess as the children sat on a chair on either side of him.

"Didn't I promise to tell you how the *Martyrs' Mirror* was made?" Father asked the children.

"Yes, Father, you promised!" said both

children.

"Bring the book to me," said Father. "Bring me the new one with the light brown cover and bring me the old, old one with the big clasps."

The books were so heavy that Lois Ann and Paul could hardly carry them. First Father took the big one with the clasps. He opened it in the middle.

"Oh, look at the funny writing," said Lois Ann. "I can't read it."

"That is not funny writing," Father replied. "That is German. Great-grandfather can read it well. I can read a little, but I can read this new one much more easily.

"Long ago many Christians who believed the Bible, had to suffer. They did not want to have the minister baptize their little babies. They did not believe that communion bread becomes the body of Jesus. They believed we should love our enemies, that only Christians should be baptized, and that communion bread is not Jesus' body, but only helps us to remember Him. You remember how Dirk Willems and Hans Brael and Little Joost had to suffer. In this martyr book are many stories like these.

"Once there was no book like this. Then one day long ago a man in Holland thought that he would like to put the stories of these Christians into a book. Some stories he remembered. Others he heard from his friends. Some were written in books and kept in libraries. Others were written on animal skins and kept in court houses. For many years he copied these stories. At last he had many pages of papers with stories on them. He took these true stories to a printer who printed them on paper and made many large books. These books were printed in the Dutch language. The people in Holland could read them.

"In America many Christians loved the Bible and tried to obey it every day. They were called Mennonites. These people were very unhappy because there was war in America.

" 'We wish we had more martyr books,' they said. 'We want our boys and girls to read these true stories. It may help them to want to follow Jesus too. We want them to love their enemies. We do not want them to go to war. But these books are in Dutch. Our boys and girls cannot read Dutch, but they can read German.'

"Some one thought of Peter Miller. They knew that Peter Miller could read Dutch and German and other languages. Some men went to Peter Miller and asked him if he would write the whole martyr book in German. Peter said that he would do it.

"Every day Peter Miller worked on the martyr book. He got up early in the morn-

ing before daylight. He sat at his table
until late at night working by candlelight.
Always he was writing the martyr book.
He worked many years. His hair became
white and his face wrinkled. One day
Peter Miller finished the work.

"Then the big printing press at the
Cloisters began to run. Up and down it
went, printing the martyr book on big

sheets of paper. The sheets were cut and made into books. Leather covers with big clasps were put on the books. Many Mennonite people read these books. This old book with the big clasps is one of the old, old books that was made when Peter Miller lived in the Cloisters."

"Was the new book made then too?" Paul asked.

"Oh, no," Father said. "After a long, long time more and more Mennonite children learned to speak English. They could read English much better than they could read German. Some could not read German at all.

"Then these people said, 'If we want our boys and girls to know about these men and women who died for Jesus, we must have an English martyr book.'

"They found a man who could read Dutch well. He took the Dutch martyr book and wrote it in English. He worked three years, and at last the work was done. Some day you children will be able to read these stories in the martyr book for yourselves. They are wonderful stories of men and women and boys and girls who loved Jesus more than anything else in the world, even more than their own lives."

The Children's Easter

It was Easter morning. Out on the green lawn tiny blue and pink and white Easter flowers were blooming. On the living room window was Mother's Easter lily with its great white blossom and its beautiful shining green leaves. Mother was singing as she set the table for Sunday morning breakfast:

"Jesus Christ is risen today, Alleluia!
Our triumphant holy day, Alleluia!
Who did once upon the cross, Alleluia!
Suffer to redeem our loss, Alleluia!"

Before the family went to the breakfast table they all sat in a circle in the living room. Father held his Bible in one hand and when Mother had brought Baby Ruth into the living room he began to sing:

"Jesus Christ is risen today, Alleluia!
Our triumphant holy day, Alleluia!

Who did once upon the cross, Alleluia!
Suffer to redeem our loss, Alleluia!"

Father and Mother and all the children
helped to sing this beautiful Easter song.
Then Father opened his Bible to Luke 24.
Mother opened her Bible to Luke 24 and
Lois Ann helped Paul to find the place in
his Bible. She found the place in her own
Bible. Baby Ruth had a little New Testament and opened it as if she were going to
read, too. All the family read together the
beautiful words from the Word of God, the
story of the first Easter morning when
Jesus arose from the dead. Then Father
asked Lois Ann to tell the story. This is
what she said:

"Very early one morning a little group of
sad women went out to the grave of Jesus.
They wanted to put sweet spice on His
body because they loved Him so much.
But when they came to the grave they
found that the stone was rolled away from

the door of the grave. They looked into the grave but Jesus was not there anymore. The grave was empty. They did not know what to do.

"Then two beautiful angels appeared dressed in shining clothes. The women were afraid and bowed their heads far down to the earth. Then the angels talked. They said, 'Why do you hunt for the living among the dead? Jesus is not here. He is risen as He said He would do. He told you He would die and be buried and rise again.'

"Then the women remembered what Jesus had said and they knew that the words of the angel were true. They left the grave and told Jesus' disciples that an angel had talked to them and had told them that Jesus had risen. But the disciples thought it could not be true.

"Then Peter ran out to the grave and looked down and saw that only the clothes lay in the tomb. Jesus was not there. He was surprised too at this wonderful thing.

"Late that afternoon Jesus met two people as they were walking along the road to their home. They invited Him to supper and when Jesus blessed the bread and broke it and gave them some, they knew that it was Jesus. Then Jesus disappeared."

After Lois Ann had finished her story, the children knew that it was time to pray. They knelt down at their chairs and prayed quietly as Father prayed aloud to God. Father thanked God for Jesus who died for us, and he thanked God that Jesus arose from the grave on Easter morning. He thanked God that Jesus lives today in the lives of Christians and that Jesus lives in heaven, too. Then he prayed for the minister who would preach in the church that morning and for all the people who would come to church. He prayed for Mother and Lois Ann and Paul and Baby Ruth, too. When the prayer was finished Father said, "Amen."

"What does 'Amen' mean?" asked Lois Ann softly as she walked beside Father to the breakfast table.

" 'Amen' means that I believe that God is going to answer my prayer," Father said. "When you say 'Amen' it means that you believe God will answer your prayer."

At breakfast that morning Father talked to the children about the Sunday school lesson. The children always liked breakfast on the Lord's Day because they always talked about God and His Word. Lois Ann and Paul knew that Father and Mother loved the Word of God very dearly and wanted them to love it too. Father told them that morning that they would have communion in church that day and that church would last a little longer.

"What is communion?" Paul asked.

"I will tell you about it this afternoon," Father promised. "Try to listen carefully when Brother Weaver preaches this morning and tell me this afternoon what you have learned about communion."

Lois Ann and Paul tried hard to please the Lord in Sunday school. They said their verses when the teacher asked them to and they listened well in story time. On the board in front of the room the teacher put a large paper picture of a tomb. In front of the tomb she put a big stone. Then she put two beautiful angels on either side of the tomb. She had pictures of the women who came to the tomb and of Peter and John. Even though the children had heard the Easter story many, many times, they wanted to hear it again. They knew that Bible stories are the most wonderful stories in all the world and that all of them are true. When Sunday school was over, the children sang,

"Jesus Christ is risen today, Allelulia!
Our triumphant holy day, Alleluia!
Who did once upon the cross, Alleluia!
Suffer to redeem our loss, Alleluia!"

When the song was over the children walked in neat rows into the church. Lois saw Mother and Baby Ruth sitting on the one side of the church with the mothers. On the other side Paul saw Father sitting with the big boys' class. Soon Lois was sitting beside Mother and Paul was sitting with Father. The minister was reading from the Word of God. The Church was quiet while the minister read. Sometimes a baby would coo or make a little sound, but no one talked. Everyone listened to what God said to them from the Bible. When the minister had finished reading, all the people knelt at the benches to pray to God. They closed their eyes and talked quietly to God in the church and God listened. Even though all over the world, people were talking to God at one time, still God heard every prayer, even little Paul's prayer.

When the people had finished praying, the minister opened his Bible and read a verse. He did not read from the big open Bible that always lay on the minister's desk but from his own Bible that he loved so much. He talked about Jesus and about how Jesus died for us. He talked too about the last supper that Jesus ate on earth and how He said that the bread should make us think of Jesus' body and that the wine should make us think of His blood.

Lois Ann watched very quietly when the deacon took a tray covered with a clean white cloth and a pitcher and a cup from inside the desk. While all the people in the church stood, the bishop prayed that the Lord would bless them. When the prayer was finished he said the very same words that Jesus had said,

"Take, eat. This is my body which is broken for you. This do in remembrance of me."

He broke off a little piece of bread and gave one to the minister and one to the deacon. Then he gave a little piece of bread to each Christian in the church. Very quietly each person ate his piece of bread. Then the deacon poured the grape juice from the pitcher into the large cup and gave it to the bishop. Again all the people in the church stood and bowed their heads while the bishop asked the Lord to bless the people as they drank from the cup. Again all the people sat down and the bishop handed the cup to each Christian. While the people drank from the cup, all sang beautiful songs about the cross. Lois Ann and Paul helped to sing the songs. One of the songs was:

"What can wash away my sin?
Nothing but the blood of Jesus."

Still the service was not over. When the deacon read from the Bible the story of how Jesus washed His disciples' feet, Lois Ann and Paul listened carefully. All the people of the church listened. Some of them had their heads bowed and their eyes shut, and Lois Ann knew that they were praying. Soon men came in with little tubs of water and clean white towels. Very quietly the people would go to the tubs. On the women's side two women would go together. Mother sat down and Aunt Ida quietly washed her feet and wiped them with the towel. Then Aunt Ida sat down and Mother washed her feet and wiped them with the towel. All the women and girls at church that morning who were Christians did this. All the men and boys who were Christians washed feet too. When everyone had finished, the bishop asked them all to stand for the benediction. Then all the people sang:

"Praise God from whom all blessings
    flow,
Praise Him, all creatures here below,
Praise Him above, ye heavenly host,
Praise Father, Son, and Holy Ghost."

Church was over, and soon all the families were in their cars driving towards home. Father and Mother were very quiet

on the way home because they were thinking about Jesus. Lois Ann and Paul felt
very happy as they looked at the fresh
green fields and heard the robins singing
their spring songs.

"Isn't this a joyous Easter, Father?" said
Paul.

"Yes, it is," Father answered happily.

An Easter Walk

In the afternoon after Baby Ruth was awake, all the family went for a walk up the long back lane. Father pulled Baby Ruth in Paul's red wagon and Mother and the other children walked beside him. Under the walnut tree the grass was long and soft and the pine tree nearby made a long shadow because it was nearly evening. Here the family sat on the grass and Father told the children what the communion meant.

"It was the evening before Jesus went to the cross to die for us. In a room upstairs Jesus and His disciples sat around a table. Here Jesus ate the passover lamb for the last time because He was going to be the real passover lamb the next day. After the last passover supper was over, Jesus took bread and gave thanks and gave some to each of His disciples. He told them that when they ate the bread they should remember Him and think of how He died for them. Ever since that time almost all Christians eat the communion bread and think of Jesus.

"After that He gave them the cup and told them that when they drank from the cup they should remember His blood. Ever since that time almost all Christians drink from the cup and remember Jesus in a communion service."

"Are all Christians to wash feet like they did in our church this morning?" Lois Ann asked.

"Yes, God wants all Christians to wash feet," Father said. "After Jesus had given the disciples the bread and the cup he left the table and tied a towel about Himself. Then He began to wash the disciples' feet. At first Peter did not want Jesus to wash his feet, but when Jesus told him what it meant, he wanted Jesus to wash his hands and his head, too. In those days only slaves washed other people's feet. Jesus wanted to show us that we should not wish to be great people, but that we should be willing to do the things that nobody else wants to do. He said that those who do not wish to be great are happy. When we wash feet at communion time, we are telling the Lord and telling each other that we are willing to be a servant of others for Jesus' sake."

As the family walked down the hill Lois Ann and Paul were thinking about what Father told them. Suddenly Lois Ann said, "Father, is that why you didn't say anything when Mr. Smith took the best tomato plants and left the little ones for you last year? Was it because of what Jesus said that night when he washed the disciples' feet?"

Father smiled as he quietly answered, "Yes, Lois Ann. That is the reason."

The House in the Orchard

School was over and Paul and Lois Ann had gone out to play in the orchard. The locust trees were in bloom, the little green peas had their first white blossoms, and the bees were buzzing around the roses. That morning Father had looked at the thermometer and said, "Seventy degrees! It's really warm so early in the morning!"

"Oh, Father, may we go barefooted?" asked Lois Ann.

"Well, Mother, what do you think?" Father asked.

Mother looked up from the sink where she was filling round cardboard boxes with the ripe, red strawberries that John and the children had picked last evening.

"When I was a girl my father told us we could be barefooted when the locusts were blooming," she said as she smiled.

"They told us we could go when the first

peas were blooming," Father said.

"They told us we could go barefooted when we saw the first bumblebees," said John.

"Sister Plank told us they were allowed to go when the thermometer said seventy degrees," Lois Ann said.

"Father, I believe there are four reasons for the children to be barefooted today," Mother said. "I can smell the locust blossoms now. The peas in our garden are blooming. I saw a bumblebee in the yard yesterday, and you told us that the thermometer says seventy degrees, didn't you?"

"I think you should keep your shoes on your feet until we have finished picking this morning's berries. You know how tender your feet are in spring. After that you may be barefooted," Father told the children.

All that morning Paul and Lois Ann

helped to fill the boxes with ripe, red strawberries. As they filled the boxes they set them by the crates and John packed them carefully. The children's backs grew tired and they were very warm but they remembered that Father had promised them that if they would help to pick the berries for market in the morning, they could play in the shady, cool orchard all afternoon. The rows looked very long, but at last the last ripe berry was picked. The children ran into the house where Mother had a good dinner waiting for them. After Father asked a blessing, they all had a good meal of chicken and waffles with strawberry ice cream for dessert. Mother looked very tired and Father asked Paul and Lois Ann whether they would dry the dishes before they went to the orchard. Paul did not like to dry dishes, but when he saw how tired Mother was and thought about how hard she worked to give him food and clothing, he promised to help. In a short time he and Lois Ann had finished their task.

"May we go now, Mother?" they asked.

"Yes, you have worked well today. You may play until I call you for supper," Mother answered.

The children ran to the orchard on the hill with its many trees full of little, hard green apples. They swung for a while on the big rope swing Father had put under the Summer Rambo tree. Then they climbed the Smokehouse apple tree that had branches like steps. They looked into the deep hollow hole in the Ben Davis tree where the fat red hen was sitting on a nest of eggs. They wondered how the baby chicks would ever get out of their tree house. Then they went up to the raspberry patch at the far end of the orchard, and ate some of the warm, sweet, red raspberries. At last they began to play house under the old Baldwin apple tree.

"I wish we had a real house under this tree," said Paul. "We could build a house with wood and potato sacks and play that it is a real house."

"But we are too little to build such a house," said Lois Ann. "Do you think Father would help us?"

"Let's ask him," Paul said.

That evening the children told Father of their plans. Father laughed and said, "We had a wood and burlap bag house when I was a boy. Some day when it is raining and I cannot work in the fields I will help you to make a frame for the house. Aunt Rachel helped to build our house when we were children. Perhaps she would help you to sew burlap bags together for walls for your house. She is coming to help Mother next week, you know. Perhaps Mother can spare her."

The children waited and wished for a

rainy day. At last one Thursday morning Lois Ann awoke to hear the music of the raindrops on the tin roof outside her window. Father and Mother were not up yet and Lois Ann lay very still in her room waiting until she heard Father going down the steps. Soon she heard Mother walking softly past her door so she wouldn't waken Baby Ruth. Lois Ann tiptoed down the steps. Paul's door was still shut, for he hadn't heard the raindrops' song on the roof.

"What is my little girl doing up so early?" Father asked as he lifted Lois Ann away up to the ceiling.

"Father, do you remember what you promised Paul and me?" Lois Ann asked.

"Yes, I do, and as soon as the milking is finished and breakfast and family worship are over, I will help you to build your house. Perhaps Mother will want to help too. She could show you how to sew the bags together for the walls."

That morning in family worship, Lois Ann thanked God that she had a kind father who would help them to build a playhouse. Under the big Baldwin apple tree the ground was still dry and not many raindrops came through the shiny leaves. First Father took his shovel and dug four holes to form the corners of a square. Then he got four strong rails from the pile back of the woodshed. While Paul held one rail steady in one hole, Father shoveled ground all around it, stamping it hard with his shovel and his feet. They did this with the four rails forming four posts, one at each corner. Then Father got four pieces of wood just a little longer than the space between the posts. He nailed one end of the board to the top of one post and the other end to the top of the next post. He did this with each board.

Then he told Lois Ann to get some old

baling wire from the junk pile. Paul helped Father stretch the bent wire into long straight pieces. Father stretched the wire from one board to another crosswise to make the roof frame. He stretched more wire lengthwise over the roof. He told Paul and Lois Ann to go with him to the barn floor. Father got six old burlap bags. He placed straw on the straw cutter and cut it fine, while Paul and Lois Ann filled the bags with straw. Father told them that this would be the tent roof. Then with a big bag needle and some cord that Mother had saved from the store Father sewed the ends of the bag shut. They laid the flat bags of straw across the baling wire above the tent and laid flat stones on the bags so that the wind would not blow them away.

Now the roof was strong and water-proof, but the house had no sides. Just then Lois Ann saw Mother and Baby Ruth coming to see the new house. Paul had gone for some old burlap bags to make sides to the house. Quickly Father ripped the string from the sides, making eight large pieces of burlap. He nailed the burlap to the roof boards and to the poles at the sides. There were two pieces on each side. Mother took the big bag needle and sewed the burlap together to make the wall. In the front they left one piece of burlap hanging loose to make a door. Here Father put a big stake to form one side of the door frame. The other side of the frame was the pole at the corner. The children decided to let the door open always so that the house would be light. They got orange crates from the woodshed for tables and a stove. They set orange crates on end, one above the other.

"I think our house should have a yard," said Paul that evening, "because when the cows are in the orchard in early spring they might chew up the wall of our house just as Billy chewed Lois Ann's handkerchief. Cows like to chew bags."

"That is easy," said John. "I will drive a few tall stakes in the ground for posts and we will string baling wire from stake to stake. That will be your fence. The cows won't come in then."

"But what will we use for a gate? We don't want to crawl under our fence. We need a new gate."

Mother had the answer. "How would the end of that old iron bed that is in the woodshed do for the gate?" she asked.

John said it would be just right. Next evening when he came in from cultivating corn, John took the ax and twelve strong stakes. He drove them into the ground with quick, heavy blows. Then he and Paul and Lois Ann stretched three rows of baling wire from post to post. While the children held the end of the old iron bed steady on an orange crate, John fastened it to the stake with hinges he made of wire. He made a loop of wire to hook over a nail on to the stake. "That is your latch," he told the children.

Mother gave the children a rose bush to plant in their yard and they planted other flowers there, too. Sometimes their house was a store. Sometimes it was a farm house. Sometimes it was the school where Lois Ann taught her dolls and Baby Ruth. The children soon had a path worn to the orchard house.

Mother often told the children that we do not need many toys to make us happy, but that often we can have the best time with things that we have if only we are wise enough to know how to use them.

The Buffalo Boy and the Rice Girl

One Sunday afternoon Lois Ann was very sleepy. She buried her head deeper into the soft pillow as she lay on the big studio couch in the kitchen. Suddenly she heard the sound of car wheels rolling across the fine stones in the barnyard. Quickly she ran to the window. Paul was already running down the barn hill to meet Aunt Caroline who was getting out of the car.

"Oh, Aunt Caroline," cried both the children. "We are so glad you came."

Aunt Caroline walked between Paul and Lois Ann to the front door where Father and Mother were waiting for her. Everyone was glad to see Aunt Caroline, for she was always happy. She was a teacher and she loved children. She could tell the best stories, Lois Ann thought.

As soon as Mother had put Aunt Caroline's coat in the closet, both the children said, "Aunt Caroline, will you tell us a story?"

"Perhaps Father and Mother do not want to hear a story," said Aunt Caroline. "Perhaps they want to talk about many other things."

"Yes, we do want to hear a story," said Father. "Mother and I like your stories as much as the children do."

Aunt Caroline sat on the big studio couch in the kitchen. At her right side sat Paul and at her left side sat Lois Ann. Father sat in his big rocker by the window and Mother sat on her low chair by the lamp.

Aunt Caroline smiled as she began her story.

Subagio is a boy almost as big as Paul. He lived in Java with his sister, Suwarni, and his father, mother, grandfather, grandmother, aunt, and a big cousin. Subagio sleeps on a mat on the floor of the house. All the rest of the family sleep on mats on the floor too. Often in the evening Subagio and Suwarni tell each other what they have done and seen and heard during the day.

These children do not talk about school because they do not go to school. Father and Mother do not have enough money to buy books, tablets, pencils, and school clothes. Because they do not have much money, the children must work every day. Do you want to hear about their work?

When it is time to plant rice, Suwarni is very busy. She must carry the rice plants to the women who plant the rice. The rice plants are always muddy because they have grown in seed beds of mud. Suwarni's dress is wet and is very muddy. But she does not care because her wet dress keeps her cool. The women are happy while they work, and that makes Suwarni happy too. Three or four times a year Suwarni must help to plant rice for several days. Some of the women plant so fast that it looks as if they were only reaching their hands in and out of the water. The women will be paid with some rice when it is ripe.

Suwarni's other work is picking seeds from kapok in a factory. The best kapok in the world comes from Java. But she does not like this work, for the kapok gets into her hair. Then her hair is hard to comb. It gets into her eyes too, and into her nose and makes her sneeze. Suwarni does not know what kapok is used for. Today it is mostly used to make mattresses and upholstery.

Kapok grows on trees in pods that look like milkweed pods. Men and women have long bamboo poles with knives on the end. With these knives they cut the pods.

Then they put them in baskets. At the factory Suwarni helps to take out the seeds and the soft kapok is dried. When the fiber is dry, it becomes large and soft. It looks like popcorn popping. Then the kapok is put in bales and sent far away to make pillows. The seeds are cleaned. From the seeds comes some oil which is used in cooking.

Subagio's work is different. His work is to take care of the water buffalo. Subagio takes four buffaloes out to a place where they can find grass or rice to eat. If they eat grass by the side of the road, Subagio watches the cars and trucks that are going by all day long. He must keep the buffaloes from walking on the road. Some days they roam over the rice fields where the rice has been cut. On days when Father or one of the owners must use a buffalo, Subagio has only two or three buffaloes to watch. When Subagio gets tired,

he climbs on to the back of a buffalo and lies down. The buffalo walks very slowly and sometimes Subagio falls asleep on his back.

If Subagio meets another buffalo boy, they will stop and talk a while. One buffalo boy has a pet bird that always goes along with the buffalo. The bird eats rice, and sometimes he flies about with the other birds. But he always comes back to sit on the head or on the back of one of the buffaloes.

When the sun begins to hide behind the tall palm trees, Subagio drives the buffaloes to the nearest canal. The buffaloes go into the water and Subagio washes them with a brush of long grass. When they are clean, Subagio takes his bath, too. He splashes about, making all kinds of movements. He puts his head all the way under the water. When he has finished, he puts on his trousers, picks up his whip and chases the buffaloes home.

At home, he finds Suwarni waiting for him. They eat their supper of rice, dried fish, and red peppers. They play a few games with the other children after supper. Then they go to the bamboo house and talk until they fall asleep.

"That is a good story," said Lois Ann.

"I would like to try riding on the back of

a water buffalo," said Paul.

"I think you should use your kapok mattress instead," said Father smiling.

Sosan

Sosan is a smiling, friendly little Indian girl. Whenever anyone passes her house she calls out, "Salaam." Her friends call back to her, "Salaam." Then she is happy and smiles and shows her pretty white teeth.

Sosan has two brothers and two sisters. Her brothers are older than she is and her sisters are younger. Sosan's oldest brother is not her real brother, but she loves him just the same. One day, before Sosan was born, some people brought a tiny baby to the mission hospital. He was very weak and thin. The Indian Christian preacher asked Sosan's father and mother if they would like to take the baby. They were happy to do this. Now the tiny baby has become Sosan's big brother. When Sosan grows older she will understand that her father and mother were very kind and helpful when they took this baby. Sosan's father and mother taught the baby about Jesus. Perhaps if they had not taken him he would never have known that Jesus loves him.

Sosan lives in a mud house. But the house is not wet or sticky, as you might think. One time, when the house was being built, the walls were wet and sticky. But in India there is much sunshine. The hot sun soon made the walls dry and hard. There are five rooms in Sosan's house. One room is the kitchen; one is a storeroom; one is a bedroom; and one is her father's workroom. Can you guess what the fifth room is? It is the place where the cows and chickens live. Yes, it is like a barn, but it is part of Sosan's house.

Sosan's father is a tailor. He has a sewing machine and makes clothes for other people. He also makes pretty dresses for Sosan and her sisters. Sometimes Sosan and her brothers try to help their father.

Just across the road from Sosan's house lives the Indian preacher. In front of his house there is a big bell. Every Sunday morning an old man rings this bell. When Sosan hears the bell she knows that she must get ready for Sunday school. She washes her face and puts on one of the pretty dresses which her father has made for her. Her mother combs her hair and makes two braids. Then her mother goes to the storeroom and takes out a handful of rice and puts it in Sosan's dress pocket. This is Sosan's Sunday school offering. Sometimes her mother will give her a pice (a penny) instead of rice, but many times she gives only rice. When the collection basket is passed Sosan puts all the rice into the basket. Then all the boys and girls sing, "I have given rice and pice for Jesus." Perhaps you wonder how rice can be used for Jesus. Well, the Sunday school teacher

sells the rice and puts the money in the
Sunday school offering. This year the boys
and girls of Sosan's Sunday school are giving money for Bibles for the people of
Tibet. The people of Tibet are not Christians. Giving them Bibles is one way to tell
the people of Tibet about Jesus.

Sosan goes to a Christian day school just
as you do. Her mother is a Christian. Her

teacher teaches her Bible stories. The school is not a very big one. One time many Hindu boys and girls also came to the school, but now they go to their own school. The Hindu boys' and girls' parents do not like their children to study in a Christian school, so they started their own school. This made the missionaries feel very sad.

There are only four grades in Sosan's school. After the boys and girls pass fourth grade they must go forty miles away from home to go to school. There all the boys live together in one big room and all the girls live together in a big room. Sometimes the children get homesick and lonesome. Don't you feel sorry for them? You can pray for them.

Preacher Pedro

"Isn't there one person here who needs Jesus?" asked the minister.

Fifteen-year-old Pedro sat very still. *Surely the man beside me can hear my heart beating,* thought Pedro. Still his heart beat louder and louder.

As Pedro walked out of the church, he wanted to talk to the minister. When he came to the door where the minister stood, he looked straight into the eyes of the minister. But there was no time to talk. Everyone wanted to get out. As Pedro looked into the minister's eyes, the minister said, "Pedro, I am going to pray for you tonight."

Pedro passed through the crowd and slipped away from everyone else. His heart was warm and happy because the minister would pray for him tonight. He thought about that all the way home from church. He thought of many other things, too. He wondered how he could be a Christian in his home. His father lived with another woman and his mother was a gambler. His grandfather and grandmother and brothers and sisters did not know anything about the Bible.

Still Pedro knew that God was calling him. He knew that he should give his heart to Jesus. He did not know just what God wanted him to do, but he wasn't afraid.

Next evening Pedro went to church again. As soon as the invitation song began, Pedro stood and confessed Jesus before everyone in the church.

That night Pedro thought and thought. He knew that he would have to talk with his mother. He wanted to help his mother become a Christian and to make his home a Christian home.

Next morning, very early, he came

downstairs to the kitchen where his mother was starting the fire to make coffee. The smoke made big circles above his head and passed out through the big cracks in the wall. He leaned against the stove. Then he said, "Mama, I accepted Christ as my Saviour last night. Mama, I have a big work to do now."

"Ay! Pedro, what do you mean? Now your grandfather and grandmother will be angry. What did you have to do?"

"I didn't do anything but take Christ as my Saviour, Mama. I knew that I was a sinner. When I opened my heart, Jesus came in. Now I feel all clean inside." Then Pedro said, "Mama, I want our home to be a Christian home. We should read the Bible every day. I will begin to read the Bible to you."

"Oh, Pedro, you will make trouble. I know that your grandfather and grandmother won't listen to the Bible," said

Mother.

"I am not afraid, Mama. We will see what will happen. I will pray to God about it, and He will take care of it all."

"I will pray to the virgin to help you, Pedro," said his mother.

"Mama, the virgin is dead. The Bible tells us that the virgin thanked God for Jesus. She needed a Saviour, too."

"What Pedro? The virgin did not need a Saviour. She was holy. What is this new religion you have?" said Pedro's mother.

"I know how you feel, Mama, but wait until you see. You will understand better when you hear what the Bible says," Pedro answered.

Every evening Pedro read the Bible to his mother, his brothers and sisters and his grandfather and grandmother. Then he prayed. This is what he said in his prayer, "O Holy Father, bless our family and help the rest to understand what Thy Word says. Make our home a Christian home. Help us to accept Thee into our hearts. Bless Mother and help her to understand that Thou art God, and that Jesus is her only Saviour. Amen."

Sunday came and Pedro thought, how can a Christian home have gamblers in the house? I must speak to Mama again. That afternoon Pedro said to his mother,

"Mama, I want to ask you to do something else. Will you tell the gamblers today that they can't come into this house anymore? A Christian home should not have gamblers in the house."

"Well, Pedro," said his mother, "I don't know. You see the gamblers give me twenty-five dollars every Sunday. We need the money very much."

"What do we do with that money, Mama? Do we have a better home because we have it?" asked Pedro.

"Well, no. We do not have better food

and clothing since we have the money. I
will try to do as you say. If you want to be a
real Christian, I do not want to make it
hard for you," said Pedro's mother.

Then Pedro asked his mother one more
thing. He said, "Mama, do not be angry
with me. Will you promise me that you
will not smoke any more? A Christian
home ought not to have people who

smoke."

"Well, Pedro, what are you going to ask next?" laughed his mother. "I do not know how I can stop smoking, but I will try."

Now Pedro was much happier. The gamblers were gone, and his mother did not smoke in the house anymore. But still he was not altogether happy. Every night he read to the family from the Bible. He read near the little oil lamp which was their only light. Every day his mother watched the life of her son, who had changed so much. She knew that he had something that she did not have. She began to want what he had.

One day Pedro begged his mother to go with him to church. At once she was willing to go. All Pedro's brothers and sisters went to church too. Pedro's mother listened to the new and wonderful story of Jesus. She wanted to go to church again and again. One night Pedro's mother thought, "Pedro does not have something in his heart. He has Someone."

That night Pedro's mother invited Jesus to come into her heart. Pedro had never been so happy in all his life. God had answered his prayer. Mother was a Christian.

How happy Pedro was! How he like to hear his mother pray. He liked the motto his mother put on the wall. It said, *"No smoking in this house. This is a Christian home."*

"Now we have a home in which Jesus will want to live," said Pedro.

Every day Pedro trusted in God more, and every day he believed more and more that God answers prayer. His grandparents became Christians too. He prayed and hoped that God would save his father too. Sometimes his father went to church with him.

Day by day Pedro became more bold for

the Lord. He liked to help in the church. One Sunday afternoon he took tracts to the people who lived far up in the hills. He went to prayer meeting too.

At first, Pedro's family only went to church on Sundays. Mama and his grandparents did not understand why they needed to go to prayer meeting too.

But Pedro wanted to go. "Mama," he said, "it is a prayer meeting and I believe in prayer. I want to learn to pray better. I will go."

Soon he convinced his whole family to go along to prayer meeting every week.

Everywhere Pedro went his light shone brightly. He was not ashamed to be a Christian. He talked so much about Jesus that people called him "Preacher Pedro."

Pedro only smiled and said, "Some day I hope I will be a real preacher."

How Rachel Grew

Sister Smith often stopped by the grocery store at the corner of Maple and Market Streets. The store owner was a Jewish woman. She had two sons, Joe and Albert, and a baby girl named Rachel.

When Sister Smith first saw Rachel, she was so little she could not say a word. She would only smile and open her big blue eyes very wide when Sister Smith smiled and talked to her.

But Rachel did not stay little. Every day she drank her milk and her orange juice. Every day her blue eyes grew brighter. Soon her little hands could hold her toy rabbit with the long ears. One day a white tooth appeared in her mouth. Another day when her mother came to her carriage, Rachel smiled and said, "Mama." Soon she could say many other words.

Sister Smith enjoyed watching Rachel

as she grew and grew. When Rachel was four years old, Sister Smith wished she could take her to Sunday school. But Rachel was a Jewish girl, and her mother did not want her to go to a Christian church. Often Sister Smith prayed that God would help Rachel's mother and that Rachel could come to Sunday school.

One Sunday morning Sister Smith had a big surprise. Rachel's mother and brothers were going to spend the day at their Uncle Jacob's house. Albert brought his little sister, Rachel, over for Sister Smith to keep and told her that mother said she could take Rachel along to Sunday school. How happy Sister Smith was that she could take Rachel to Sunday school that morning.

After that, Rachel often came to Sister Smith's house. Sometimes she would look at the pictures in the Sunday school papers and Sister Smith would tell her about

Jesus. But Rachel could not talk to her mother about Jesus. One day when Rachel was in third grade she said to Sister Smith, "Don't tell my mother that I talk about Jesus at your house. Joe goes to the Jewish synagogue. They don't believe in Jesus, but I believe in Him."

Sister Smith answered, "Joe does not believe in Jesus because he does not know who Jesus is. We must pray for Joe that he will learn to know who Jesus is and that he will love Him too."

Rachel bowed her head and shut her eyes tight and said, "Pray for Joe now."

Next summer Rachel went to a Christian home with many other Jewish girls. One day something happened. Rose, who was Rachel's good friend, lost her coat in a large crowd of people. There were so many people that Rose could not find her coat anywhere.

It was soon bedtime and time for prayer. When Rachel's turn came she prayed that Rose's coat would be found. Soon the telephone rang. When Sister Jones went to answer, she heard a voice saying, "The lost coat has been found. You may call for it tomorrow."

"God has answered my prayer. God has answered my prayer, " Rachel said again and again.

One day Rachel told Sister Smith that

God had taught her something new. She said, "Last year in school one of the girls told me to tell my teacher a lie. I knew that it was wrong. But when I heard you talk to God and pray in the name of Jesus, I knew that He would forgive me. I don't have to go to the synagogue once a year to ask God to forgive me."

Rachel was only ten years old, but she knew more about God than many men and women know because God was her teacher.

The Passover

Many years ago God's people were slaves in Egypt. King Pharaoh said that he would not let the people go. But God is stronger than any king.

God said to Moses, "I will free you and all My people. At midnight I will go through all the land of Egypt. The first-born boy in every home in Egypt will die, but there will be a way for all the first-born Jewish boys to live. I will give you a sign. Tell the Jews to take a good, strong lamb and kill it. Do not take a sick lamb or a lamb with sores. Take the lamb's blood and put it in a dish."

"Take a bunch of hyssop and dip it in the blood. Put the blood on the two side posts of the door and over the top of the door. Do not leave your houses until morning. When I see the blood, I will pass over you. Not one Jewish boy will die. I will free all of My people."

When the king saw that the boys were dead, he was frightened. He said to Moses, "Take your people and your animals and leave this land."

How glad the people were to leave the land. Many, many people left Egypt that night. There were grandfathers, grandmothers, fathers, mothers, brothers, sisters, and little children. They had sheep and cows. They had clothing and they even had bread which was not yet finished. How glad they were because God had made them free.

On and on they went until they came to the Red Sea. There they saw mountains on each side of the sea. Some of them were afraid, but they remembered that God had said, "I will free you."

Back in Egypt King Pharaoh thought and thought. Then he grew very angry because God's people had gone. He called

his men together and told them to go with him and to help him to bring the people back. Moses looked back and saw the king and his men coming. Then God talked to Moses. He said, "Tell the children of Israel to keep on going, and the people of Egypt shall know that I am the Lord."

There were God's people. In front of them was the Red Sea. On each side were the mountains. Behind them was the angry king. Suddenly a great cloud came between the people of God and the people of Egypt. This cloud was dark on the side of the king and his people, and light on the side of Moses and God's people.

Then God spoke again. This time He told Moses to hold his rod over the Red Sea. Moses did what God told him to do, and God sent a strong east wind that blew all night long. It rolled the waves back and made the sea dry land. There was a path for God's people to walk on, and on either side of the path God made, the waters were piled high like a wall.

The king's people could not see because the cloud made everything dark for them. When the last of God's people had crossed the path in the sea, the cloud disappeared. The king and his people came in their chariots. Then God said to Moses, "Put out your rod over the sea again."

As soon as Moses did this, the waters rolled back and covered all the Egyptians. None of them escaped.

Ever since the time when God make His people free, some Jewish people have kept the Passover. All the family sit around a table and eat the Passover food. They pray and are joyful because they remember how God delivered them.

What do you think the Jewish people eat at the passover? Everything which they eat tells them of something that has happened.

First they have a paste made of apples. This paste is the color of bricks and it tells the people that long ago God's people had to make bricks for the king.

Then they eat horse radish. This is so bitter that it makes the tears flow. Then they think of how bitter the life of God's people was in Egypt. Next they look at the egg which is covered by a shell. This egg is to make them think of a man in the grave and of how God's people were like a man in a grave in Egypt.

The salt water makes them think of the salt waters of the Red Sea and of how they came out free and alive while the king and his men were killed.

What does the bone of the lamb on the table mean? This tells the people of the lamb that had to be killed so that the oldest boy would not have to die. They do not know that the lamb was to tell of Jesus who had to die so that we would not have to die.

His blood saves us from death.

The bread on the table is very flat and looks more like crackers than like bread. It tells of the bread that they baked after they left Egypt.

On every Passover table there is a lighted candlestick. This tells the family that light shone in the houses of God's people while there was only darkness in the homes of the people of Egypt. Today we know that Jesus is the light which shines on the darkness of sin.

On the Passover table there is always a special cup which is called Elijah's cup. The youngest boy in the family must go to the door and open it for Elijah. All the family looks for Elijah to come in and tell them that Jesus is coming. But Elijah never comes. Jesus has already come to free us from sin.

On the table is green parsley too. This tells of springtime when there is fresh new life on the earth. When the children of God left Egypt, God brought them to a new life. We think of spring as Easter time, the time when Jesus arose to give us new life.

At the Passover table all the family listens as Father reads the story of how God freed His people from the king of Egypt. Then the youngest boy or girl of each family asks the Father four questions. First he asks, "Why is this day different from all other days of the year?"

Father answers, "On all other days we eat leavened bread, but this night we eat only unleavened bread."

Then the child asks, "Why do we eat all kinds of herbs all year and on this day we eat only bitter herbs?"

"We are reminded of the bitter days when we were slaves in Egypt," replies Father.

Then the child asks the third question,

"Why do we this night dip onions into the salt water?"

Father says, "To make us think of crossing the Red Sea and of the sorrows we left behind."

Then the child asks the last question, "Why do we rest on a pillow at the Passover table?"

"God freed us from the king of Egypt with a strong arm. In God alone is our rest," Father says.

The Jewish people think mostly of the past at Passover time. They do not know that Jesus came to take their sins away. God wants us to tell the Jewish people that Jesus has come to free them from sin.

Zefania and the Snake

Whiz-whiz-whiz went the bicycle wheels down the sandy path. Zefania's long, strong, black legs pedaled fast, for it was a long way to the outschool. His heart was so full of love for the Lord Jesus that he had gotten up early. Perhaps it was at the second crowing of the rooster that he left his bed so that he could go to Omuga and tell the people there about our wonderful Saviour. Zefania did not know that two persons were watching him as he rode down the path. The risen Lord, Who dwelt in Zefania's heart by faith, was making him joyful and glad that morning. The devil, who hates the Lord, did not want Zefania to go and warn the people about sin.

One mile, two miles, six miles, twelve miles, fourteen miles, and then suddenly Zefania saw something in the road, right

before him. Because he had not time to
stop he rode right into it. He fell from the
bicycle and got tangled with a soft body. It
was a big snake, a cobra. It was very angry
about being disturbed in his morning nap.
The bicycle had hurt the snake. He struck
with his fangs at the man and at the bicycle. Poor Zefania's foot was caught in the
bicycle, and he couldn't get away from that

frightful snake. But he knew he must get away and slowly he pulled himself along. Then he was able to free his foot and crawl along leaving the cobra and the bicycle in the path. By and by the cobra slid into the grass by the side of the path and Zefania saw him no more.

Zefania stood on his feet again. "Well," he thought, "I have been bitten by that cobra and I shall die. But there is no one near to whom I can tell that I was bitten by a snake. When they find my body they will not know what happened to me. I think I shall write a note telling about the cobra. I'll write that the one who finds my body shall tell the missionaries about it. Then they will come and take my body back to the station and bury it there." Zefania got out his pencil and paper.

Then he stopped. "I will see where that cobra bit me. I do not feel sick yet. I feel well."

Zefania looked at his hands. There was no mark. He looked at his feet. There was not a scratch. He felt his face. "I don't believe that the cobra has bitten me," thought he. "I am all right. Praise the Lord! He promised to care for His people. I shall get up and ride on to the church and preach the Gospel."

Whiz-whiz-whiz went the bicycle. Zefania thanked God for saving him. Fifteen miles, twenty miles, twenty-four miles, twenty-seven miles, Zefania rode. Then he saw the little church made of sticks and mud. A grass roof kept out the rain. Little black boys and girls smiled happily as Zefania propped his bicycle by the side of the church. Mothers with babies tied on their backs were happy to see him. Big, strong men shook his hand.

They went into the church and sat on the mud-brick seats. They prayed and they praised the Lord with many songs.

Then Zefania preached the Word with great boldness. The devil was not happy. He had wanted to keep Zefania from telling others about the Lord Jesus. But the Lord did protect him from snake bites just as He said He would. Find the verse in Psalm 91 in which the Lord promises to protect His people from snakes. The snake is sometimes called an adder in the Bible.

A Boy and His Dream

One day Joseph's father gave him a new coat. The coat was very beautiful with many different colors. The red stripes were as red as the flowers that grew in the fields around the shepherds' tents. The blue was as blue as the sky above on a clear summer day. There were other colors too, just as bright and as beautiful. But Joseph's brothers did not have such beautiful coats. When they saw Joseph wearing his coat, they were angry and hated Joseph.

Something else made the brothers angry, too. Often Joseph would dream at night. One day he said to his brothers, "Last night I had a strange dream. I saw a field with many sheaves of grain. The sheaf that I had made stood up straight in the field, but the sheaves that you had made bowed down to my sheaf. I had another dream, too. The sun and moon and eleven stars bowed before me."

Then Father Jacob said, "What is this dream that you have dreamed? Shall I and your mother and brothers come to bow ourselves to you?"

Jacob thought of Joseph's dream a long time. He did not forget it. But Joseph's ten brothers did not like the dream and they were very angry about it.

Soon the ten brothers drove their flocks of sheep and cattle out to new fields to find grass. They had been gone many days, when Jacob said to Joseph, "I want you to go out to the place where your brothers are tending the sheep and see how they are getting along."

It was a long way to the valley where the brothers were feeding the sheep. As Joseph was walking in a field looking for his brothers, he saw a man who said, "What are you looking for?"

"I am looking for my brothers. Please tell me where they are feeding their flocks," said Joseph.

"They have gone on farther, for I heard them talking about it," said the man.

On and on Joseph went until he came to the place where the sheep and goats were feeding. When his brothers saw the boy coming and wearing his beautiful coat,

they said,

"Look. This dreamer is coming. Let us kill him and put him in a pit and say that a wild animal has eaten him. Then his dreaming will stop."

But Reuben said, "No, don't kill him. Put him into the pit, but don't hurt him."

Reuben thought that sometime he would help Joseph to get out of the pit and send him home to his father.

As soon as Joseph came near to his brothers, they took his pretty coat from him. Then they carried Joseph out to the pit in the valley and threw him into it. It was an empty pit with no water in it. Then Joseph could hear his brothers walking away.

While Joseph was alone in the pit, his brothers were eating their meal of bread. As they sat there, they looked up and saw camels far away. As the camels came closer, they saw that they carried loads of spices and sweet perfumes. They knew that the Arab drivers were going to Egypt with their loads of spices and perfumes. Judah thought of a new plan. He said, "Why should we kill our brother and hide our bad deed? Let us sell Joseph to these men, for he is our brother."

The other brothers thought that Judah had a good plan. They went to the pit and drew Joseph out of the pit. They took him to the Arab drivers and sold him for twenty pieces of silver. But they kept Joseph's beautiful coat.

Later Reuben came to the pit to help Joseph. He was surprised to find that Joseph was gone. Tearing his clothes for sorrow, he went to his brothers and said, "Joseph is gone. Where shall I go?"

Then the unkind brothers did another bad thing. They took Joseph's beautiful coat and dipped it into the blood of a young goat which they had killed. This coat they sent back to poor old Jacob. As soon as Jacob saw the coat, he knew it and thought that Joseph was dead.

"It is my son's coat," he said. "A wild animal has eaten him. He must be torn to pieces."

Then Jacob tore his clothes and put on ugly clothing. For many days he was very sad. His sons and his daughters tried to cheer him, but it seemed that Jacob would never be happy again.

Many years passed. Jacob was an old man now with many grandchildren and some great-grandchildren. Still no one had heard anything of Joseph. Times were very hard because the crops did not grow. Every day the grain became less and less, and still no more grain grew in the fields. Then Jacob said to his ten sons, "Don't be angry with each other. I have heard that there is corn in Egypt. Go to Egypt and buy corn for us so that we may live and not die."

The ten men said good-bye to their father and to their wives and children and went down the road toward Egypt. When they went into the governor's house, they were met by a man who asked them many questions. When this man knew that they had a younger brother, Benjamin, at home with his father, he told them to go home and bring their youngest brother. To make sure that the brothers would do this he said he would keep one of them named Simeon in prison until they would return. After giving them grain, he let them go.

The grain lasted many days. But one day when nearly all the grain was gone, Jacob told his sons to go to Egypt again and buy grain.

"But we cannot go without Benjamin," said Judah. We may not even see the man if we do not bring Benjamin," he said.

"Why did you tell the man you had a

little brother?" asked Jacob.

"We didn't think he would tell us to bring him. We only answered his question," Judah said. "But please send the boy with me. I will take care of him, and if I do not bring him back to you, you may do with me whatever you wish to do. We could have been gone and have returned already if we had not waited so long."

"If there is no other way, you may take Benjamin," said Jacob. "Take also a present of honey, spices, nuts, and perfume for the man and be sure to give him the money you found in your grain bags last time."

Benjamin and his brothers were on the way many days. When they arrived in Egypt, they were told to come into the governor's house. They remembered the money that they had found in their grain bags and they were frightened.

"We found the money in our bags at the

inn where we spent the first night. We didn't know how it came there," the man explained to the governor's servant.

"Don't be afraid. Your money came to me," said the servant, "but come, for you are invited to dinner at the governor's house."

At dinner the governor again asked many questions. He seemed to like little Benjamin for he talked very kindly to him. Simeon was there too. By next morning the brothers were ready to go. They had not gone very far on their way home when one of the king's servants came running to them, and told them that the governor's silver cup was missing.

"We are very sure that we do not have the cup," said the brothers. "Do you think that people who brought back money they found in their bags would steal the governor's silver cup? You may kill any one of us in whose bag you find it."

Quickly the men took down their bags and opened them. The servant looked into each bag. When he looked into Benjamin's bag, there was the silver cup. Tearing their clothes, the men got on their donkeys and rode back to the city. The governor came out and told them that they had stolen the cup. The brothers said that they would all be willing to be slaves, but the governor said, "No, you may all go, except the one in whose bag the cup was found."

Then Judah walked up to the governor, "Please, let me say something. The other time we were here you asked us whether we had a father or a brother. We told you that our father was an old man and that we had a little brother, whom Father loved very much. You asked us to bring our brother next time but we told you that we could not take him away from Father, because then Father would die. Then you said that if we did not bring him along, you would not let us see your face again.

"When we had no more food, Father told us to come here to buy more. We told him that we could not come without Benjamin. Father said that he could not bear to see Benjamin go. Then I promised Father that I would bring him back or bear the blame myself. Please let me stay here as a slave, and let the boy go home. I can't go to Father without the boy."

Suddenly the governor said to his servants, "Tell all the people except these strangers to go out of the room."

When they had all gone, the governor said to the brothers, "I am Joseph. Is Father still living?"

The brothers did not answer a word. They were so frightened.

Then Joseph said kindly, "Please come near to me. I am Joseph, your brother, the boy you sold. Don't be sad because you sold me. God has sent me here to save

many lives. There have been two years of
famine, when no food would grow. There
will be five more such years. God sent me
here to save your lives. It was not you who
sent me here but God. I am now ruler of all
the great land of Egypt. Go to Father, and
tell him that Joseph is the ruler of all
Egypt. Tell him to come here, too. Tell
him not to wait. You may all come to live in

this land. I will give you food all the years of the famine. Tell Father everything and bring him down to me."

When Joseph had finished talking, he threw his arms around Benjamin and cried. Benjamin cried too. Then Joseph kissed all his brothers and put his arms around them and cried. After that the brothers were not afraid to talk with Joseph.

When the brothers came home they had a wonderful story to tell Jacob. It was the story of Joseph. At first Jacob could not believe the story, but the sons showed him the wagons Joseph had sent to bring them all to Egypt. Then Jacob said, "It is enough. Joseph is still alive. I will go and see him before I die."

One night while Jacob was on his way to Egypt God told him not to be afraid to go to this strange land. God promised that He would go along with him and that He would bring him back. He promised him that he would see his son Joseph. Now Jacob was even more happy.

How glad the family was that they could all be together again! Joseph gave them a good place where they could live with their families. They were all happier than they had ever been before. Joseph greeted them kindly and they liked to have him help them. Joseph's dream had come true.

Indian Children

Where we go to school each day
Indian children used to play,
    All about our native land
    Where the shops and houses stand.

And the trees were very tall,
And there were no streets at all
    Not a church and not a steeple
    Only woods and Indian people.

Only wigwams on the ground
And at night bears prowling round.
    What a different place today
    Where we live and work and play!

Reprinted by permission of the publisher (J. B. Lippincott Company, Copyright 1919), from FOR DAYS AND DAYS by Annette Wynne.

The Wonderful World

Great, wide, beautiful, wonderful World,
With the wonderful water round you
    curled,
And the wonderful grass upon your breast,
World, you are beautifully dressed.

The wonderful air is over me,
And the wonderful wind is shaking the
    tree.
It walks on the water, and whirls the mills,
And talks to itself on the tops of the hills.

You friendly Earth, how far do you go,
With the wheat-fields that nod and the
rivers that flow,
With cities, and gardens, and cliffs and
isles,
And people upon you for thousands of
miles?

Ah! you are so great, and I am so small,
I hardly can think of you, World, at all;
And yet, when I said my prayers today,
My mother kissed me and said quite gay,
"You are more than the earth, though you
are such a dot:
You can love and think, and the earth can-
not!"

Fairest Lord Jesus

Fairest Lord Jesus! Ruler of all nature!
O Thou of God and man the Son!
Thee will I cherish, Thee will I honor,
Thou, my soul's glory, joy, and crown!

Fair are the meadows, fairer still the
woodlands
Robed in the blooming garb of spring;
Jesus is fairer, Jesus is purer
Who makes the woeful heart to sing.

Fair is the sunshine, fairer still the moon-
light,
And all the twinkling starry host;
Jesus shines brighter, Jesus shines purer,
Than all the angels heaven can boast.

Christian Light Publications, Inc., is a nonprofit conservative Mennonite publishing company providing Christ-centered, Biblical literature in a variety of forms including Gospel tracts, books, Sunday school materials, summer Bible school materials, and a full curriculum for Christian day schools and homeschools.

For more information at no obligation or for spiritual help, please write to us at:

Christian Light Publications, Inc.
P. O. Box 1212
Harrisonburg, VA 22801